Learning Alfresco Web Scripts

Learn a powerful way to successfully implement unique integration solutions with Alfresco

Ramesh Chauhan

BIRMINGHAM - MUMBAI

Learning Alfresco Web Scripts

First published: November 2014

Production reference: 1311014

Published by Packt Publishing Ltd.
Livery Place
35 Livery Street
Birmingham B3 2PB, UK.

ISBN 978-1-78439-060-0

www.packtpub.com

Credits

Author
Ramesh Chauhan

Reviewers
Snig Bhaumik

Dhaval Joshi

Bernd Krumböck

Piergiorgio Lucidi

Commissioning Editor
Dipika Gaonkar

Acquisition Editor
Kevin Colaco

Content Development Editor
Priyanka Shah

Technical Editor
Nikhil Potdukhe

Copy Editors
Relin Hedly

Deepa Nambiar

Project Coordinator
Kartik Vedam

Proofreaders
Simran Bhogal

Maria Gould

Ameesha Green

Paul Hindle

Indexers
Mariammal Chettiyar

Rekha Nair

Tejal Soni

Production Coordinator
Arvindkumar Gupta

Cover Work
Arvindkumar Gupta

About the Author

Ramesh Chauhan is presently working as a lead consultant at CIGNEX Datamatics. He has core IT experience of around 9 years. Having strong expertise in Alfresco, he has implemented and delivered customized business solutions in Alfresco for customers across the globe and has extensively used Alfresco in multiple production projects. He earned his Bachelor of Engineering degree in Information and Technology from Nirma Institute of Technology, Gujarat University, India. He also contributes to Alfresco community forums.

Acknowledgments

I would first like to extend my gratitude to Lord Swaminarayana and my guru, H. H. Pramukh Swami Maharaj, for all the blessings. I would like to thank my mom and dad for their unconditional love and support. Special thanks to my loving and caring wife, Priyanka Chauhan, who has always encouraged me and supported me throughout the journey of this book. Big thanks to my one-year-old daughter, Misri, who has been the source of inspiration for me.

I would like to thank Packt Publishing for this opportunity. I would like to thank all the technical reviewers for their valuable feedback and give my thanks to Kevin Colaco, Priyanka Shah, and Nikhil Potdukhe from the Packt Publishing team. It was really nice working with the entire Packt Publishing team. I sincerely appreciate Priyanka Shah, the content development editor, and Nikhil Potdukhe, the technical editor, who helped a lot in fixing my writing style with their valuable feedback.

I would like to thank our management team at CIGNEX Datamatics for encouraging me to write this book as a part of the community contribution from our organization. My sincere thanks to Mr. Munwar Shariff (CTO, CIGNEX Datamatics) for all his support. I would also like to thank the entire Alfresco practice team at CIGNEX Datamatics for being very supportive. Thanks to Aadit Majmudar for helping me whenever needed while writing this book. I would like to thank Dhaval Joshi especially, who has been my very good friend and colleague at CIGNEX Datamatics. He has always been with me whenever I needed his help and input. Thanks to him and my friend, Chirayu Joshi, for believing in me, supporting me, and motivating me to write this book.

About the Reviewers

Snig Bhaumik is the Technical Director at InfoAxon Technologies Limited (www.infoaxon.com) and is responsible for designing solutions for content and knowledge management powered by open source technologies. He has diverse experience of over 13 years in open source technologies such as Alfresco, Liferay, and Pentaho, and Microsoft .NET.

Snig's areas of expertise include knowledge management, collaborative content management, business process automation, social networks, business intelligence, search, and emerging technologies. He acts as a senior consultant on many projects, driving BI, KM, and ECM agendas with senior stakeholders. He is a sought-after speaker in these areas and also writes regularly in the form of white papers and blogs. His works can be accessed at http://blog.infoaxon.com/, http://onalfresco.blogspot.in/, and https://github.com/SnigBhaumik/.

He has a lot of experience in delivering open-source-powered solutions to global customers in the fields of international development, social housing, construction, banking, retail, and insurance. He is an active participant in various open source communities and has contributed functionalities to some of the leading open source platforms.

As an open source enthusiast, Snig is an active contributor to several open source communities:

- He has authored *Alfresco Cookbook 3, Packt Publishing* (http://www.amazon.com/Alfresco-3-Cookbook-Snig-Bhaumik/dp/184951108X)
- He led the development and management of the roadmap for Alfresco add-ons on Alfresco and InfoAxon's marketplace (http://www.infoaxon.com/solutions/addons/#all)
- His key add-ons released on Alfresco include:
  - Bootfresco (https://github.com/SnigBhaumik/Bootfresco)
  - Calendar Event Participant (https://addons.alfresco.com/addons/calendar-event-participant)

- ° Alfresco Category Browser (`https://addons.alfresco.com/addons/category-browser`)
- ° Task Document Previewer (`http://www.infoaxon.com/add-on/task-document-previewer/`)
- ° Content Uploader Pro (`https://addons.alfresco.com/addons/content-uploader-pro`)

- He manages projects at Google Code for the open source portlet for Twitter in Liferay (`http://code.google.com/p/liferay-twitter-portlet/`)
- He manages projects at Google Code for the open source portlet for Facebook in Liferay (`http://code.google.com/p/liferay-facebook-portlet/`)
- Alfresco ECM (he is the author of the Alfresco Calendar components that are now included and distributed in Alfresco Version 3.0)
- He solely manages the Liferay Portal practice at InfoAxon
- He is one of the key stakeholder and technical decision maker of the Pentaho BI business stream at InfoAxon

Dhaval Joshi has more than 10 years of experience in software development. For the past 6 years, he has been working with Alfresco. He has executed more than 10 projects in Alfresco and more than five projects in different Java-based open source technologies. He is also an Alfresco-recognized Alfresco developer.

He has huge experience in providing open source content management enterprise solutions. He has written more than 100 Alfresco web scripts for different clients in various projects.

He has huge experience in Alfresco DM, WCM, Share, DAM, and the Record Management system. He also has expertise in customizing and extending Alfresco. Other than Alfresco, he has good experience in CMS/WCM such as OpenCMS, CQ5, and Documentum.

Bernd Krumböck is a self-employed IT professional. In the last 7 years, he has implemented and supported many projects for the NGO/NPO Volkshilfe NÖ (NPO for nursing and other services with about 1,000 employees in Lower Austria). One of these projects is a document management system based on Alfresco, which is needed for an ISO standardization process. As a result, he has become the new maintainer of the Oracle Server support for the Alfresco Community extension.

Besides this, he is working on various business applications that are mainly based on Java/J2EE. However, his skills are also used for server, database, and network administration.

A few years ago, he was employed as a system administrator at REWE Group, Austria. His principal task was the administration of the HP-UX, Linux, and Oracle database systems. During this time, he contributed various code to CUPS and other projects.

In his free time, he works on various small projects that extend his smart home system. One of these projects resulted in a Linux kernel driver for a USB CAN adapter from 8 devices (`https://github.com/krumboeck/usb2can`).

Piergiorgio Lucidi is an open source Enterprise Content Management (ECM) specialist and a certified Alfresco trainer at Sourcesense. Sourcesense is a European open source systems integrator providing consultancy, support, and services around key open source technologies.

He works as a mentor, technical leader, and software engineer, and has 10 years of experience in the areas of ECM and system integration. He is an expert in integrating ECM solutions in web and portal applications.

He regularly contributes to the Alfresco community as an Alfresco Wiki Gardener. During Alfresco DevCon 2012 in Berlin, he was named the Alfresco Community Star.

He contributes to the Apache Software Foundation as a PMC member and committer of Apache ManifoldCF and is the project leader of the CMIS, Alfresco, and Elasticsearch connectors. He is a project leader and committer of the JBoss community. He also contributes to some of the projects of the JBoss Portal platform.

He is a speaker at various conferences dedicated to Java, Spring Framework, open source products, and technologies related to the ECM and WCM world.

He is an author, technical reviewer, and affiliate partner at Packt Publishing. For Packt Publishing, he has co-authored *Alfresco 3 Web Services, Ugo Cei*, and *GateIn Cookbook, Ken Finnigan and Luca Stancapiano*. As a technical reviewer, he has also contributed to the books *Alfresco 3 Cookbook, Alfresco Share*, and *Alfresco 4 Enterprise Content Management Implementation*, all published by Packt Publishing.

As an affiliate partner, he also writes and publishes book reviews on his website Open4Dev (http://www.open4dev.com/).

I would like to thank Packt Publishing for another great opportunity to contribute to a project dedicated to the Alfresco platform.

---

www.PacktPub.com

Support files, eBooks, discount offers, and more

You might want to visit www.PacktPub.com for support files and downloads related to your book.

Did you know that Packt offers eBook versions of every book published, with PDF and ePub files available? You can upgrade to the eBook version at www.PacktPub.com and as a print book customer, you are entitled to a discount on the eBook copy. Get in touch with us at service@packtpub.com for more details.

At www.PacktPub.com, you can also read a collection of free technical articles, sign up for a range of free newsletters and receive exclusive discounts and offers on Packt books and eBooks.

http://PacktLib.PacktPub.com

Do you need instant solutions to your IT questions? PacktLib is Packt's online digital book library. Here, you can access, read and search across Packt's entire library of books.

Why subscribe?

- Fully searchable across every book published by Packt
- Copy and paste, print and bookmark content
- On demand and accessible via web browser

Free access for Packt account holders

If you have an account with Packt at www.PacktPub.com, you can use this to access PacktLib today and view nine entirely free books. Simply use your login credentials for immediate access.

"This book is dedicated to my daughter, Misri, for being my source of inspiration, and I would like to present this to her as a gift on her first birthday."

Table of Contents

Preface

The first thought that came to my mind when I got the opportunity to write this book was whether I will be able to take this up or not, as implementing web scripts in projects is completely different from writing a book on it. However, at the same time, I was curious and excited as well to write my first book. What I always believe is—if you think you can do it, then just go for it and give your best try to achieve it. Hence, I took this opportunity and started my new journey of writing my first book to share my knowledge, learning, and experience with you.

To give you a brief account of the book, web scripts is one of the key features of Alfresco and is a must know for each and every developer working on Alfresco. It is really essential for a developer working on Alfresco to be familiar with the powerful web script framework and understand how to practically implement web scripts. In this book, you will get to learn all the basic details required to work with web scripts in Alfresco and get yourself competent with web script development for your projects to implement useful integration solutions with Alfresco.

A few years back, I was also a beginner. Now, I have vast experience of using web scripts in different real-time business implementations. Based on my learning and experience from my journey as a beginner to my current level of expertise in regards to implementing web scripts, I have tried to provide the most useful information that will help a lot to new or experienced developers who are looking forward to exploring and learning about web scripts.

I have attempted to share the knowledge and learning that I have gained throughout my experience working on Alfresco web scripts. I have tried to explain the key concepts about web scripts in a simple way and have used practical examples to understand how to implement web scripts. I have also gone deep into technical details where I felt it would be required to help you learn about the web script framework in a better way.

By the end of this book, you will be able to say that you are familiar with web scripts and are ready to take up new assignments to develop custom web scripts as you have gained the required knowledge to practically implement them in Alfresco. You will also be able to debug, troubleshoot, and fix the issues that you might come across while working on web scripts. Also, you will be able to share the core technical knowledge about the powerful web script framework with your colleagues.

My journey of writing this book has reached its destination as the book is now available in your hand. Now, you are about to begin your journey of reading this book and learning about Alfresco web scripts. Hope you have a wonderful journey ahead!

What this book covers

Chapter 1, *Getting Familiar with Web Scripts*, introduces you to web scripts by exploring answers to some of the basic questions about web scripts, which will give you a clear idea about how web scripts can be useful for implementing integration solutions with Alfresco.

Chapter 2, *It's Time for the First Web Script*, walks you through implementing your first web script in Alfresco, which will give you the knowledge required about the core fundamentals along with some key points to take care of when practically implementing web scripts in your projects.

Chapter 3, *Understanding the Web Script Framework*, covers the powerful web script framework, which will make you well acquainted with the detailed technical knowledge of web script execution and the backbone pillars of the web script framework.

Chapter 4, *Building Blocks of Web Scripts*, provides you complete details about all the components to build web scripts.

Chapter 5, *Invoking Web Scripts*, describes the various ways you can execute a web script that will help you to choose the way to execute web scripts as required.

Chapter 6, *Creating Java-backed Web Scripts*, helps you understand how to practically implement Java-backed web scripts through the implementation of a sample use case.

Chapter 7, *Understanding JavaScript-based Web Scripts in Detail*, explains what you can do with JavaScript APIs in Alfresco web scripts and makes you aware about the different root objects to access these APIs and useful root objects exposed by the web script framework. It also takes you through some code examples for some of the common functionalities in JavaScript-based web scripts.

Chapter 8, Deployment, Debugging, and Troubleshooting Web Scripts, guides you through the options to deploy web scripts in detail and also walks you through some useful debugging techniques and troubleshooting pointers along with some important points to execute web scripts in a production environment.

Chapter 9, Mavenizing Web Scripts, gives you basic knowledge of setting up the development environment in Eclipse using the Alfresco Maven SDK to develop web scripts.

Chapter 10, Extending the Web Script Framework, familiarizes you with the possibility of extending the core components of the web script framework in Alfresco to help you understand the power of working in an open source technology.

What you need for this book

You will need to have a working instance of Alfresco that will help you throughout the journey of this book. You should use Alfresco Version 4.2 and above.

Who this book is for

If you are a new Alfresco developer and are exploring web scripts in Alfresco, then this book is for you. This book will help you gain the key basic knowledge required to implement web scripts in Alfresco. If you are an experienced developer in Alfresco and are familiar with the basics of web script development but have not yet fully explored the web script framework, then this book is for you as it will help you gain the required knowledge about it. If you have already explored web scripts in Alfresco and have gained a very good understanding about it, then you will find this book useful as a quick and handy reference.

Conventions

In this book, you will find a number of styles of text that distinguish between different kinds of information. Here are some examples of these styles, and an explanation of their meaning.

Code words in text, database table names, folder names, filenames, file extensions, pathnames, dummy URLs, user input, and Twitter handles are shown as follows: "`DeclarativeWebScript` sets the response to be rendered."

A block of code is set as follows:

```
private RestTemplate restTemplate;
public void setRestTemplate(RestTemplate restTemplate) {
   this.restTemplate = restTemplate;
}
```

When we wish to draw your attention to a particular part of a code block, the relevant lines or items are set in bold:

```
<html>
  <body>
    <p>Hello! ${args.name}.</p>
  </body>
</html>
```

Any command-line input or output is written as follows:

```
curl -u admin:admin "http://localhost:8080/alfresco/service/
helloworld?name=Ramesh"
```

New terms and **important words** are shown in bold. Words that you see on the screen, in menus or dialog boxes for example, appear in the text like this: "Click on the **List Web Scripts** link."

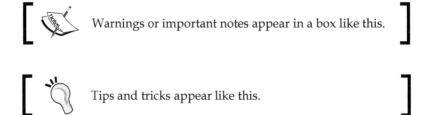

Warnings or important notes appear in a box like this.

Tips and tricks appear like this.

Reader feedback

Feedback from our readers is always welcome. Let us know what you think about this book—what you liked or may have disliked. Reader feedback is important for us to develop titles that you really get the most out of.

To send us general feedback, simply send an e-mail to feedback@packtpub.com, and mention the book title via the subject of your message.

If there is a topic that you have expertise in and you are interested in either writing or contributing to a book, see our author guide on www.packtpub.com/authors.

Customer support

Now that you are the proud owner of a Packt book, we have a number of things to help you to get the most from your purchase.

Downloading the example code

You can download the example code files for all Packt books you have purchased from your account at http://www.packtpub.com. If you purchased this book elsewhere, you can visit http://www.packtpub.com/support and register to have the files e-mailed directly to you.

Errata

Although we have taken every care to ensure the accuracy of our content, mistakes do happen. If you find a mistake in one of our books—maybe a mistake in the text or the code—we would be grateful if you would report this to us. By doing so, you can save other readers from frustration and help us improve subsequent versions of this book. If you find any errata, please report them by visiting http://www.packtpub.com/submit-errata, selecting your book, clicking on the **errata submission form** link, and entering the details of your errata. Once your errata are verified, your submission will be accepted and the errata will be uploaded on our website, or added to any list of existing errata, under the Errata section of that title. Any existing errata can be viewed by selecting your title from http://www.packtpub.com/support.

Piracy

Piracy of copyright material on the Internet is an ongoing problem across all media. At Packt, we take the protection of our copyright and licenses very seriously. If you come across any illegal copies of our works, in any form, on the Internet, please provide us with the location address or website name immediately so that we can pursue a remedy.

Please contact us at copyright@packtpub.com with a link to the suspected pirated material.

We appreciate your help in protecting our authors, and our ability to bring you valuable content.

Questions

You can contact us at questions@packtpub.com if you are having a problem with any aspect of the book, and we will do our best to address it.

1
Getting Familiar with Web Scripts

In this chapter, we will cover the following topics:

- Understanding web scripts
- Reasons to use web scripts
- Understanding when to use a web script
- Understanding where web scripts can be used
- Understanding how web scripts work
- Types of web scripts

Consider a scenario where you have to work on a project to develop a customized business solution with a backend repository such as an Alfresco content management system. It is going to be an integration project with the Alfresco content repository. The end goal is to build up a business implementation that has a custom frontend application interacting with the Alfresco repository in a secure way in order to allow the end users to access the content on demand and to provide access to features of the Alfresco repository. Basically, you want to create, update, and delete content in the Alfresco repository and are interested in retrieving the required content on demand from the Alfresco repository from the custom frontend application in a secure way.

Now, you might have a lot of questions on your mind. You must be curious to find out how it is possible to access the Alfresco repository from the custom frontend application. What are the possible alternatives to access the content residing in the Alfresco repository from the custom frontend application? Is it going to be a complex implementation to build up an API accessing the Alfresco repository? Is it going to be a secure communication from the frontend application to the backend repository? How is it going to maintain the client state during the communication with the Alfresco repository in order to access, update, or delete content from the repository based on the user's access? And the list of questions still goes on…

Whenever there is a question, there is an answer. Also, the answer to all of your previous questions is **Alfresco web scripts**. Using web scripts, you can build up a customized integration solution using Alfresco as the backend content repository.

It is always a good idea when we start learning about any new topic to always start with the "5Ws and 1H". It's basically the who, what, when, why, where, and how questions. This helps us to understand the topic in a better way. In this chapter, we are going to find out the useful information about web scripts by discovering the answers to some of the basic questions such as what, why, when, where, and how. Let's start and find out the answers to them and understand web scripts in a better way.

Understanding web scripts

In order to understand web scripts in Alfresco, let's begin with finding out the answer to the question "What is a web script?" from multiple perspectives.

In simple words, web scripts can be explained as follows:

- Web scripts are powerful and extremely useful services supported by Alfresco
- They are a way to interact with the Alfresco repository securely

- They are reusable across different platforms
- Web scripts provide uniform access of the content to a wide range of client applications

In technical terms, web scripts can be defined as follows:

- They are RESTful web services

What is RESTful?

REST stands for REpresentational State Transfer, which is basically an architectural style. Well-defined and uniform access to the resources through HTTP request methods, uniquely identified resources through the URI, and representation of these resources are the key principles of REST. Any implementation following this architectural style is known as RESTful.

- They are bound to a specific **Uniform Resource Identifier (URI)**
- They respond to HTTP methods such as GET, POST, PUT, and DELETE
- They are a lightweight implementation

From a developer's point of view, web scripts have the following properties:

- They are easy to understand and learn
- They are easy to develop
- They are easy to debug
- They are easy to maintain
- They are easy to deploy
- They are faster to implement
- They would be the first choice when it comes to accessing the Alfresco repository securely from external applications

From a business user's point of view, web scripts are useful as follows:

- They bridge the gap between the business requirement and technical implementation for building up business solutions with Alfresco
- They empower Alfresco in its integration capabilities to develop useful Alfresco integration solutions with external systems
- They are a unique way to implement the integration solutions on top of the Alfresco repository
- They are the backbone of the integration solution implementation with the Alfresco repository

In essence, web scripts can be talked about as follows:

- Web scripts are built on the idea of URL addressability

- Web scripts are simply a service, mapped to a human-readable form, and developed using a piece of code as their backend implementation

- For example, in a contract management system built using Alfresco as the backend repository, you can have a web script to retrieve all the draft agreements from the repository and then display them on the custom frontend application. This repository web script to get all the draft agreements will simply be accessed through its URL. This web script will also have a piece of code in the backend to retrieve the data from the Alfresco repository to produce the results in the formats as required. The URL for this web script might look like the following:

```
/alfresco/service/contract/get_draft_agreements
```

Reasons to use web scripts

It's now time to discover the answer to the next question—why web scripts? There are various alternate approaches available to interact with the Alfresco repository, such as CMIS, SOAP-based web services, and web scripts. Generally, web scripts are always chosen as a preferred option among developers and architects when it comes to interacting with the Alfresco repository from an external application. Let's take a look at the various reasons behind choosing a web script as an option instead of CMIS and SOAP-based web services.

In comparison with CMIS, web scripts are explained as follows:

- In general, CMIS is a generic implementation, and it basically provides a common set of services to interact with any content repository. It does not attempt to incorporate the services that expose all features of each and every content repository. It basically tries to cover a basic common set of functionalities for interacting with any content repository and provide the services to access such functionalities.

- Alfresco provides an implementation of CMIS for interacting with the Alfresco repository. Having a common set of repository functionalities exposed using CMIS implementation, it may be possible that sometimes CMIS will not do everything that you are aiming to do when working with the Alfresco repository. While with web scripts, it will be possible to do the things you are planning to implement and access the Alfresco repository as required. Hence, one of the best alternatives is to use Alfresco web scripts in this case and develop custom APIs as required, using the Alfresco web scripts.

- Another important thing to note is, with the transaction support of web scripts, it is possible to perform a set of operations together in a web script, whereas in CMIS, there is a limitation for the transaction usage. It is possible to execute each operation individually, but it is not possible to execute a set of operations together in a single transaction as possible in web scripts.

SOAP-based web services are not preferable for the following reasons:

- It takes a long time to develop them
- They depend on SOAP
- Heavier client-side requirements
- They need to maintain the resource directory
- Scalability is a challenge
- They only support XML

In comparison, web scripts have the following properties:

- There are no complex specifications
- There is no dependency on SOAP
- There is no need to maintain the resource directory
- They are more scalable as there is no need to maintain session state
- They are a lightweight implementation
- They are simple and easy to develop
- They support multiple formats

In a developer's opinion:

- They can be easily developed using any text editor
- No compilations required when using scripting language
- No need for server restarts when using scripting language
- No complex installations required

In essence:

- Web scripts are a REST-based and powerful option to interact with the Alfresco repository in comparison to the traditional SOAP-based web services and CMIS alternatives
- They provide RESTful access to the content residing in the Alfresco repository and provide uniform access to a wide range of client applications

- They are easy to develop and provide some of the most useful features such as no server restart, no compilations, no complex installations, and no need of a specific tool to develop them

- All these points make web scripts the most preferred choice among developers and architects when it comes to interacting with the Alfresco repository

Understanding when to use a web script

Having understood what a web script is and the reasons for using web scripts, let's now understand when to use web scripts. When working with Alfresco, it is important to know in which scenarios web scripts can be used. Web scripts allow you to build custom URI-identified and HTTP-accessible Content Management Web services to access the Alfresco content repository, and hence they can be used in various kinds of implementations to build useful business solutions with Alfresco content management systems.

In development projects:

- You can use web scripts to develop business implementations integrating Alfresco with external applications

- You can develop customized web scripts as per your business requirement

- You can leverage on the out-of-the-box web scripts available in Alfresco wherever they fit in your custom implementation

In support projects:

- Web scripts could be your savior when you are working on a support or maintenance project to maintain the live system for your customers that is built on Alfresco and has millions of records.

- You might come across a range of issues, for example, updating existing content to fix some data issues, deleting some unneeded content, getting the required content matching with the criteria specified by the business team, and so on. Web scripts can be used in such scenarios to serve these purposes.

- On a live production system, it is not possible to restart the server, and restarting a server could impact the business of a customer. Consider a scenario where you need to fix some critical issues on a production system and you are looking for an option to have the issue fixed without restarting the server. The powerful feature of web scripts to interact with the Alfresco repository without restarting the server will help you in this case, and you can fix some critical issues using web scripts to provide a good content management experience to the business users.

In general, web scripts can be used in all kinds of solutions, such as:

- Integrating Alfresco with external applications that can communicate with Alfresco using HTTP

- Developing JSR-168 portlets to build up UI services

- Developing data services

- Providing feeds for repository content

- Alfresco integration with Office

- Developing Facebook applications

- Building UI components in Alfresco SURF

Understanding where web scripts can be used

Now, it's time to understand where web scripts can be used. There are a number of different environments from where a web script can be accessed and used.

In different environments:

- They can be used from an HTTP client such as a web browser and HTTP client APIs

- It is also possible to access web scripts in JSF pages

- They can be used in JSR-168 portals

- They can be used from Facebook applications

- Web scripts can be used in the Alfresco SURF platform as well

Understanding how web scripts work

Web scripts in Alfresco mostly use the model-view-controller pattern. However, it isn't mandatory to follow this pattern all the time. The way MVC pattern works in web scripts is as follows:

- **The controller** is responsible for performing the required business logic as per the business requirement. After processing the business logic, controller populates the **model** object with the required data. Once this is done, controller will then forward the request to the **view**.

MVC in web scripts

The model-view-controller pattern in web scripts is explained as follows:

- The controller is a server-side JavaScript or Java class or it could be both as well
- The model is a data structure object passed between the controller and view
- The view is a FreeMarker template that is responsible for generating the response in the required format

The mapping of the web script URI to the controller is done through a descriptor file. It is mainly an XML file that will have the required details for a web script such as URL, description, arguments, transaction, authentication, and response formats.

Response formats are mapped to FreeMarker templates through naming conventions. For example, a FreeMarker template that returns an HTML response will have the extension `html.ftl`.

Web scripts are registered and executed by the web script engine in Alfresco.

 A descriptor, optional controller, and one or more FreeMarker response templates collectively make a web script in general scenarios. All these components are tied together through a specific document naming convention.

Making web scripts work

To make web scripts work, it is important to deploy the web script files at an appropriate location.

The descriptor file and the FreeMarker template as per the response format for a web script can be either placed on a filesystem or put into the Alfresco repository.

If a JavaScript-based controller is used for a web script, then it could be placed along with the descriptor and FreeMarker template on a filesystem or in the Alfresco repository.

If a Java-based controller is used for a web script, then the class file for the controller must be available on the class path.

 There are two types of controllers available for web scripts: JavaScript-based controllers and Java-based controllers. It is possible to have none of them, either of them, or even both of them for a web script.

Types of web scripts

There are two types of web script in Alfresco: Data web scripts and Presentation web scripts.

Data web script

Data web scripts provide an interface to the repository for the client applications to create, retrieve, update, and delete content/data in the repository. These web scripts typically send the response in formats such as XML and JSON, and client applications will have to parse it in order to use it further.

Data web scripts encapsulate access and modification of content/data residing in the repository. These web scripts are provided and exposed by the Alfresco repository server only.

Presentation web script

Presentation web scripts can be used to build user interfaces such as dashlets for Alfresco explorer, dashlets for Alfresco share, portlets for a JSR-168 portal, a UI component within Alfresco SURF, or a custom application.

These kinds of web scripts generally render HTML responses.

It is possible to host these web scripts on a separate presentation server or they can also be exposed by the Alfresco repository server.

Presentation web scripts generally make a call to Data web scripts in order to get the required data from the repository.

> Out-of-the-box web scripts available in an Alfresco installation can be found at `ALFRESCO_HOME\tomcat\webapps\alfresco\WEB-INF\classes\alfresco\templates\webscripts\org\alfresco`, where `ALFRESCO_HOME` is the base directory where Alfresco is installed.
>
> If you are using Alfresco Community 5, you can find out-of-the-box web scripts under the `alfresco` package inside `alfresco-remote-api-*.jar`, which is available at `ALFRESCO_HOME\tomcat\webapps\alfresco\WEB-INF\lib`.

Summary

In this chapter, we gained a better understanding of web scripts through some of the basic questions about web scripts. We learned what web scripts in Alfresco are, why they are the preferred choice of developers, when and where we can use web scripts, how web scripts work, and also the different types of web scripts available in Alfresco.

In the next chapter, we are going to do a hands-on exercise to learn how to implement our first web script in Alfresco.

2
It's Time for the First Web Script

In this chapter, we will cover the following topics:

- How to create a simple web script in Alfresco step by step
- The implementation of the first web script
- Extending the first web script to add a controller
- What happens behind the scene of a web script hit
- The most important things for any web script

It's now time to practically implement your first web script in Alfresco and get more familiar with Alfresco web script implementation. This chapter will help you get a clear understanding on how to create a simple web script in Alfresco, how to extend web script with controller implementation, and some fundamental things about web script implementation that are very important to know while working on Alfresco web scripts.

Consider a scenario where you are managing the project execution of developing an integration solution of a custom frontend application with Alfresco as backend repository. Now, you have been allocated a new developer to develop Alfresco web scripts who is not very familiar with web script implementation and you want to get him up to speed for web script development. Never mind, you can have him read through this chapter and he should be able to get a good understanding of developing web scripts in Alfresco after reading this chapter.

Creating your first web script in Alfresco

Whenever we start learning about any new programming language, the first program we implement is the "Hello world" program wherein we simply print the text **Hello world** as the output of the program. We will also do the same thing here. We will create a basic web script in Alfresco that will simply display **Hello world!** as the output of the web script.

In order to create a basic and simple web script in Alfresco, you will need to have a descriptor for the web script and a FreeMarker template to render the output of the web script.

Web scripts can be created from the available Alfresco user interfaces or you can have them developed outside of Alfresco and then deploy them. As we are going to implement a very basic web script here, we will use the Alfresco user interface option and will create a web script. You can either use Alfresco Explorer web client or Alfresco Share UI for this. However, as Alfresco Explorer is now not being encouraged to be used in general as it is not on the roadmap of Alfresco as no new implementations are being made in support of Alfresco Explorer, we will also not use Alfresco Explorer. Instead, we will use the Alfresco Share UI which is recommended to use in general.

Let's now create the web script. In order to create your first web script in Alfresco, follow these steps:

1. Log in to Alfresco Share UI.
2. Click on the **Repository** link from the top header.
3. Go to **Data Dictionary** | **Web Scripts Extensions**.

4. Create a new file named `helloworld.get.desc.xml` with content as follows:

```xml
<webscript>
  <shortname>Hello World</shortname>
  <description>First webscript Hello world</description>
  <url>/helloworld</url>
</webscript>
```

Downloading the example code

You can download the example code files for all Packt books you have purchased from your account at http://www.packtpub.com. If you purchased this book elsewhere, you can visit http://www.packtpub.com/support and register to have the files e-mailed directly to you.

5. Create a new file named `helloworld.get.html.ftl` with content as follows:

```html
<html>
  <body>
    <p>Hello world!</p>
  </body>
</html>
```

6. Now, hit the URL http://localhost:8080/alfresco/service/index in a browser. Provide the username and password to the authentication pop up displayed. Click on the **Refresh Web Scripts** button available at the bottom.

7. Click on the **List Web Scripts** link. You can see the **Hello world** web script by clicking on the **Browse all Web Scripts** link and search for `helloworld`.

8. Now, hit the URL http://localhost:8080/alfresco/service/helloworld. Here we go, you should see the output **Hello world!** rendered in your browser.

We have implemented the first web script in Alfresco. Now, let's try to understand what we have just done in order to implement the first web script. We first created the web script as follows:

- We implemented a GET web script to display **Hello World!** as the output

- We created the descriptor document `helloworld.get.desc.xml` for the web script

- We also created the FreeMarker template `helloworld.get.html.ftl` to render the web script response

In general, in order to create a web script in Alfresco, a minimum two files are required. One is the descriptor document and the other is FreeMarker template.

Next, we deployed the web script as follows:

- We have deployed the required files to create a web script in the Alfresco repository

- The descriptor document and FreeMarker template are placed in **Data Dictionary | Web Scripts Extensions**

> Web script files can be directly created/uploaded in the Alfresco repository in **Data Dictionary | Web Scripts Extensions** or web script files can be created and deployed on the filesystem through the code base as well.

We then registered the web script as follows:

- We hit the URL `http://localhost:8080/alfresco/service/index` and clicked on the **Refresh Web Scripts** button to register the first web script

> There are two ways to register a web script. One is through hitting the URL `http://localhost:8080/alfresco/service/index` and clicking on the **Refresh Web Scripts** button. Another way is to deploy the web script files through the code base/repository and restart the server. A server restart will also register the web scripts.

Finally, we executed our first web script as follows:

- We invoked the web script from the web browser hitting the URL `http://localhost:8080/alfresco/service/helloworld`

- The web script displayed an output as its response on a web browser

Understanding the web script URI

It is important to understand the web script URI. The way the web script URI can be represented in a generic form is `http[s]://<host>:<port>/[<contextPath>/]/<servicePath>[/<scriptPath>][?<scriptArgs>]`

The terms used in the web script URI are explained as follows:

- `http[s]`: This is the protocol to invoke the web script. This could be either `http` or `https`.

- `host`: This is the name or address of the server where the web script is deployed.

- `port`: This is the port where the web script is exposed on the server hosting the web scripts.

- `contextPath`: This is the path where the application is deployed to. For data web scripts, this would generally be `/alfresco`.

- `servicePath`: This is the path where the web script service is mapped with. Generally, this would be `/service`.

- `scriptPath`: This is the path to the web script as defined in the web script descriptor document `*.desc.xml` under the `<url>` tag.

- `scriptArgs`: These are the arguments to be passed to the web script as generally defined in the web script descriptor document `*.desc.xml` under the `<url>` tag. Arguments can be specified after the web script `scriptPath` just after `?`.

Now you understand the different terms that make up the web script URI, now you can easily understand the URI of our first web script by mapping our web script URI to the generic form of the web script URI. Note that we were not having arguments added to our first web script, hence, you would not be able to map the `scriptArgs` part. Let's now take a look at what needs to be done to add the arguments to a web script.

Adding arguments to a web script

Let's say we want to modify our first web script to display the name too in the web script response, for example, **Hello! Ramesh**. It can be done in a simple way by passing the name as the URL argument of the web script and then using this argument to generate the response in the FreeMarker template. In order to do this, we will have to perform the following steps:

1. Log in to Alfresco Share UI.

2. Click on the **Repository** link from the top header.

3. Edit the descriptor file `helloworld.get.desc.xml` at **Data Dictionary | Web Scripts Extension** location as follows:

```
<webscript>
  <shortname>Hello World</shortname>
  <description>First webscript Hello world</description>
  <url>/helloworld?name={argumentName}</url>
</webscript>
```

4. Edit the FreeMarker template `helloworld.get.html.ftl` at **Data Dictionary | Web Scripts Extension** as follows:

```
<html>
  <body>
```

```
        <p>Hello! ${args.name}.</p>
    </body>
</html>
```

5. Register the web script by hitting `http://localhost:8080/alfresco/service/index` and click on the **Refresh Web Scripts** button.

6. Now, hit the URL `http://localhost:8080/alfresco/service/helloworld?name=Ramesh` in order to execute the web script.
    On execution, you should be able to see **Hello! Ramesh.** as the output.

> It is important to understand here that even if you had not provided name={argumentName} in the third step and hit the URL to execute the web script, as mentioned in the sixth step, then you would also have got the same result. Specifying name={argumentName} in the description document helps you know about the arguments used by web script. This way, by just looking at the description document, you will know about the arguments for web script. As a good practice, you should always add the arguments used by your web script in its description document.

Extending the first web script to use the controller

The web script framework in Alfresco makes it easy to have a clear separation of concerns by following a model-view-controller pattern in order to develop a web script. All the business logic resides in the controller and it is possible to have multiple views as required to return the response in different response formats supported by the web script framework in Alfresco. The model object is a data structure used to pass information from the controller to the view. The controller populates the model object with the required data and passes it to the view to generate the response.

In the first web script, we created a basic and simple web script, which just renders the output without interacting with the Alfresco repository. Ideally, any processing related to business logic such as querying the Alfresco repository, creation of content, updating content, deleting content from the repository, and executing actions should be done in a controller. A controller could be a server-side JavaScript or a Java-based controller.

Let's extend our first web script to add a controller to get an understanding about how the controller populates and passes data to FreeMarker template and how FreeMarker template uses the model data to generate the response:

1. Log in to Alfresco Share UI.

2. Click on the **Repository** link from the top header.

3. Go to **Data Dictionary | Web Scripts Extensions**.

4. Edit the descriptor file `helloworld.get.desc.xml` as follows:

```
<webscript>
  <shortname>Hello World</shortname>
  <description>First webscript Hello world</description>
  <url>/helloworld?name={argumentName}</url>
  <authentication>user</authentication>
</webscript>
```

5. Create a new file named `helloworld.get.js` with content as follows:

```
model.email="Ramesh.chauhan@cignex.com";
```

6. Edit the FreeMarker template `helloworld.get.html.ftl` as follows:

```
<html>
  <body>
    <p>Hello! ${args.name}.</p>
    <p>email address: ${email}</p>
  </body>
</html>
```

7. Go to `http://localhost:8080/alfresco/service/index` and click on the **Refresh Web Scripts** button.

8. Now, hit the URL `http://localhost:8080/alfresco/service/helloworld?name=Ramesh` to execute the web script. It will ask for user credentials. Provide user credentials and you should see the response as:

   Hello! Ramesh.

   email address: Ramesh.chauhan@cignex.com

This is how we can have a controller added in a web script in a simple way. In the preceding example, we hard-coded the e-mail address to be returned in the web script response. We did not have any interaction with the Alfresco repository. We just populated the model object and passed it to the FreeMarker template from the server-side JavaScript controller.

Model is basically a root object that Alfresco makes available for data sharing to happen between the server-side JavaScript controller and FreeMarker template view.

You can modify the controller to get the e-mail address dynamically retrieved from the Alfresco repository based on the name argument received. With the help of Alfresco JavaScript API, you may first retrieve the user from the repository based on the name argument and then fetch the e-mail address of the user. In a server-side JavaScript controller, you can leverage on available Alfresco JavaScript API to interact with the repository. This way, we can have a web script render a response based on the data retrieved from the Alfresco repository.

In a server-side JavaScript controller, you can leverage on available Alfresco JavaScript API to access the Alfresco repository and perform business logic as required.

Behind the scenes of web script execution

Let's try to understand at a high level what happens on a web script being hit in different scenarios such as when a web script does not have a controller and when it does.

A web script without a controller

To execute the first web script we created without controller, we just hit the URL `http://localhost:8080/alfresco/service/helloworld?name=Ramesh` on a web browser, which is basically a HTTP GET request call.

All the incoming requests matching the URL pattern `/alfresco/service/*` are mapped to the web script request dispatcher servlet in the Alfresco web application configuration.

The servlet then passed the request to the Web Script Runtime to process the web script.

The Web Script Runtime passed the control to the Web Script Container. The Web Script Container internally identified which web script to execute based on the invoked web script URL, HTTP method, and the web script descriptor document `helloworld.get.desc.xml`.

We have not specified any response format explicitly in the descriptor document and have not explicitly mentioned one while executing the web script. Hence, the web script framework has rendered the HTML as the default format. Based on the naming conventions of a FreeMarker template, we recollect that we have created the FreeMarker template as `helloworld.get.html.ftl`. This generated the HTML response for the web script. The formatted response is then sent back to the web browser to display the HTML text in the web script response along with the value of the argument name.

A web script with a controller

You must have observed that in the first web script, we created the web script without the controller and then extended the web script to have the controller. The URL to invoke this web script remains the same. There isn't any difference in the URL. It was only a backend implementation that was additionally implemented to have a controller added in the web script implementation.

Behind the scenes when a web script with a controller is invoked, the web script framework in Alfresco will follow the same process as mentioned for a web script with no controller. The only difference would be before rendering the response, the web script framework in Alfresco would execute the controller implementation first. The controller will first complete the required business logic processing interacting with the Alfresco repository and generating the required data to be returned as a web script response. The controller will populate the model object to pass to the FreeMarker template.

Important things for any web script

While implementing the web scripts in Alfresco, it is essential to understand some of the very important things to be taken care of. There are three important things you should always keep in mind when developing Alfresco web scripts:

- Choosing the HTTP method for the web script
- Specifying the URL and arguments for the web script
- Response formats of the web script

HTTP methods supported by a web script

While developing web scripts and interacting with the Alfresco repository, you should ensure you select the appropriate HTTP method for the web script. It is important to understand the various HTTP methods supported by the web script framework in Alfresco so that you can select the appropriate one for your web script.

GET requests are explained as follows:

- They are used when retrieving resources from the repository
- They generally do not require a transaction
- The same HTTP GET requests return the same resource every time even after being called multiple times
- It does not have any effect on the repository as it is just a retrieval operation

POST requests are explained as follows:

- POST requests are generally used to create new resources in the repository
- Generally, POST requests send the data to the URI and expect the resource at that URI to handle the request

PUT requests are explained as follows:

- PUT requests will update the existing resource if it is present or can be used to create the new resource at a specified URI
- Like GET requests, the same PUT requests will update the same resource every time even after they are called multiple times

DELETE requests are explained as follows:

- Generally, DELETE requests are used when a resource needs to be deleted from the repository or to disable access on the resource in the repository

 It is important to understand that it is not a hard and fast rule to use the specific method for a specific type of scenario as explained for each of the previous methods. However, as a general practice, it is recommended to adhere to it.

In general for all request methods, let's take a look at some useful points as follows:

- Naming conventions of web script files make the web script framework in Alfresco interpret the type of method used for the web script.
- When a web script is executed, the web script framework in Alfresco will identify the appropriate description document, controller, and FreeMarker template for the web script based on the method used for invocation. In the first web script we created, we had .get in the filenames of descriptor document, controller, and FreeMarker template. When the "hello world" web script is executed from a web browser as a GET request, the web script framework in Alfresco identified the appropriate description document, controller, and response templates based on the method used for invocation and hence it used the ones having .get in its name.

- It is possible to define a web script with different HTTP methods. For example, in a contract management solution, you can have web scripts differentiated based on an HTTP method to create/update/delete/retrieve contract (a content based on custom content type) from the repository as follows:

  - `contract.get.desc.xml`: This gets the contracts from the repository
  - `contract.put.desc.xml`: This updates a specified contract in the repository
  - `contracts.post.desc.xml`: This creates contracts in the repository
  - `contract.delete.desc.xml`: This deletes a contract from the repository

Web script arguments

It is important to know what arguments a web script requires. As a general practice, arguments should be specified in the description document while creating the web script. Let's take a look at the two ways through which we can specify the arguments for a web script.

Explicit arguments

Explicit arguments are the ones generally provided as a query string to the web script URL. In the descriptor document, the argument name and its placeholder are generally specified as the query string in the web script URL under the `<url>` tag. For example, this is the way we have added arguments for our first web script implementation as follows:

```
<url>/helloworld?name={argumentName}</url>
```

You can have multiple arguments for the web script URL by differentiating them using the ampersand character as &amp.

 It is important to use the escaped ampersand character &amp while specifying arguments in the web script descriptor document. This is required to be done in order to ensure that web script descriptors are always a valid XML.

So for example, if you want to add another argument to our first web script, it can be declared in the descriptor document as follows:

```
<url>/helloworld?name={argumentName}&amp;organisation=
{argumentOrganisation}</url>
```

Specifying arguments in the description document is mainly to get information about the arguments required for the web script. By just looking at the description document, you can get a clear idea about what are the arguments required for the web script. If you want to specify some argument as an optional argument, you just need to add ? while mentioning the placeholder for the argument. For example, if you want to have organization as an optional argument, then you should specify it as `organisation={argumentOrganisation?}`.

Implicit arguments

This is the other way of specifying the arguments to the web script URL. In this way, the arguments are incorporated in the web script URL as shown in the following example:

```
<url>/helloworld/{argumentName}/{argumentOrganisation}</url>
```

It is also possible to have the static path in the URL after the arguments, for example:

```
<url>/helloworld/{argumentName}/{argumentOrganisation}/english</url>
```

Understanding which one to choose

- It is important to maintain consistency in the large code base of web scripts for your project; hence, you must choose the same format of specifying arguments across all your web script from a maintenance and consistency point of view.

- You could use either of the formats or you could also use both of them together based on your preferences and requirements.

Response formats for a web script

Response formats play a key role in rendering the web script response in the required format for the web script. It is important to know which response formats are supported by the web script framework in Alfresco that you can use while developing the web scripts for your business solution implementation.

Response formats supported by the web script framework

The web script framework in Alfresco supports different response formats. Here is a list of the available response formats and their mime type:

- html - text/html
- text - text/plain
- xml - text/xml
- xsd - text/xml
- atom - application/atom+xml
- atomentry - application/atom+xml;type=entry
- atomfeed - application/atom+xml;type=feed
- atomsvc - application/atomsvc+xml
- rss - application/rss+xml
- json - application/json
- opensearchdescription - application/opensearchdescription+xml
- mediawiki - text/plain
- portlet - text/html
- fbml - text/html
- php - text/html
- js - text/javascript
- calendar - text/calendar
- csv - text/csv
- xls - application/vnd.ms-excel
- xlsx - application/vnd.openxmlformats-officedocument.spreadsheetml.sheet

Specifying the response format

With the model-view-controller pattern implementation, we can have one controller implementation and multiple views. Hence, it is possible to have multiple response formats for any web script to return the web script output in different formats as requested.

You can choose any of the response formats from the supported response format lists for your web script. There are two different ways you can specify the response formats for a web script.

Specifying the response format via URL – extension on web script ID

Once you have created the required descriptor file, controller, and multiple response template documents for your web script, you can specify the response format to be used while invoking the web script URL. You can specify it as an extension of the web script ID.

For example, if there are different response format documents created for the hello world web script such as `helloworld.get.xml.ftl` or `helloworld.get.json.ftl` and while invoking the web script you want to specify XML format explicitly, then you can do this as follows:

```
http://localhost:8080/alfresco/service/helloworld.xml?name=Ramesh
```

Specifying the response format via URL – explicit format argument

Another way to specify the response format is to explicitly pass a `format` argument to the web script URL. For example, if you want to specify the XML format explicitly for the hello world web script, then you can do this as follows:

```
http://localhost:8080/alfresco/service/helloworld?name=Ramesh&format=
xml
```

The default format

While invoking a web script, if no format is explicitly specified using either of the previous two methods mentioned, then the default format as mentioned in the descriptor document will be returned. The default format can be specified in the descriptor document as follows:

```
<format default="json">any</format>
```

This indicates that the default format of the web script response to be returned is JSON and the format can be specified using either of the previous two ways while invoking web script.

If no default response format is defined in the descriptor document for a web script and also no response format is provided neither through the extension of a web script ID in the web script URL nor through explicitly specifying the format argument in the web script URL while executing the web script, then Alfresco assumes the default response format as HTML.

In general, the following are some useful points for response formats:

- Response formats are mapped to the FreeMarker template through naming conventions, for example, `helloworld.get.html.ftl` in case of our first web script

- For any web script, you can define multiple response formats such as HTML, XML, JSON, and so on.

- Based on the web script request method and requested format, the web script framework in Alfresco returns the web script response

Summary

In this chapter, we have practically implemented the simplest first web script in Alfresco, got an understanding of the Alfresco web script URI so we know how to use a web script, how to add arguments to a web script, and then extend the first simple web script to have a controller implemented.

Also, we learned at a high level what happens behind the scenes of a web script hit when a controller is used for a web script and if a no controller is implemented.

We learned some very important things while implementing web scripts in Alfresco such as different HTTP methods supported by the web script framework in Alfresco, when to choose which method, different ways of specifying arguments to a web script, a list of response formats supported by web script framework in Alfresco, and how to make your web script return a response in a different response format based on the requested response format.

Overall, we have gained a good knowledge about some of the fundamental things when implementing web scripts in Alfresco through the example of creating and extending a simple web script in Alfresco.

In the next chapter, we are going to explore the web script framework in Alfresco in detail with useful technical insights.

3
Understanding the Web Script Framework

In this chapter, we will cover the following topics:

- End-to-end execution flow of a web script
- Components that collectively make the web script framework
- Deployment architecture for a web script

The web script framework in Alfresco is a powerful one and its basic goal is to ensure that:

- Web scripts in Alfresco are easy to develop
- Web scripts can support various useful features, such as support for internationalization to render output in multiple languages, exposing configuration options for a web script, similarly like the ServletConfig for servlets

The web script framework in Alfresco is designed as per the **model-view-controller pattern** (**MVC pattern**) and makes it easy to develop new web scripts to expose a RESTful API to interact with the Alfresco backend repository.

In this chapter, we are going to deep dive into the web script framework in Alfresco to get an understanding of the various components that collectively make it a powerful framework. It is a backbone engine for registration and execution of Alfresco web scripts.

Execution flow of web scripts

Let's first understand the execution flow of web scripts in order to understand the Alfresco web script framework.

Overall flow for a web script

As soon as a request for the web script URI is hit, the execution flow of the web script gets started and continues till the request gets served with the requested response format. Let's understand the overall execution flow for a web script with a JavaScript-backed controller. The whole execution flow is as follows:

1. A request for the web script URI arrives at the web script request dispatcher in Alfresco.
2. The request dispatcher sends the request to the Web Script Runtime.
3. The Web Script Runtime delegates the request to The Web Script Container, which will first find the suitable web script for the requested URI and the requested HTTP method.
4. The next thing would be to authenticate the user first, if required, before executing the web script.
5. The Web Script Container then executes the controller implementation if available. The script processor will execute the JavaScript controller for the requested web script.

6. Controller is the core component that will interact with the Alfresco backend repository using the available set of various Alfresco services in order to process the required business logic of the web script.

7. Controller then populates the required information in the model object and passes it on to **view** in order to return the response of the web script. The result is rendered using the FreeMarker response templates. A web script can have any of the response formats as supported by the web script framework and could have multiple formats for a web script by providing appropriate response templates.

8. The task of the Web Script Container finishes and the Web Script Runtime then sends the rendered results back to the client.

9. Web script client sees the response in the appropriate requested format.

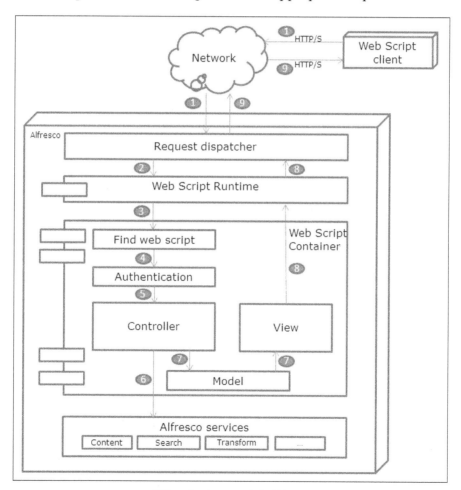

Web script framework in Alfresco

Behind the scenes implementation

As we have an overview of the overall execution flow for a web script, let's now take a detailed technical walk-through of the implementation in order to understand how a web script request gets served when a JavaScript controller-backed web script is invoked through an HTTP request from the HTTP client, for example, a web browser. You will find a lot of technical details in this section, so you might want to have a cup of coffee before you start reading this section.

As we are going to take a detailed technical walk-through in this section, you might want to have access to the source code so that it would be easy to follow while reading this section. For easy and handy access to the code, we will simply explore the JARs that are available in the Alfresco installation. You can download and install the Java code decompiler such as JD-GUI (available at http://jd.benow.ca/) that allows JAR files to be decompiled. The core classes we will get familiar within this section are mainly located in spring-webscripts-*.jar, alfresco-remote-api-*.jar, and spring-surf-core-configservice-*.jar. These JARs can be found at tomcat\webapps\alfresco\WEB-INF\lib inside your Alfresco installation directory. Once the JARs are opened in JD-GUI (decompiler), you can open the class files using *Ctrl + Shift + T* and provide the class name.

So, let's get started:

1. For Alfresco web scripts, the RequestDispatcher servlet (org. springframework.extensions.webscripts.servlet.WebScriptServlet) is configured in web.xml and mapped to the /service/* URL pattern.

2. On the first request to the /alfresco/service/* URL pattern servlet container will invoke the init method of WebScriptServlet and instantiate it with the config service (org.springframework.extensions.config. xml.XMLConfigService), Web Script Container (org.alfresco.repo.web. scripts.TenantRepositoryContainer), and authentication factory (org. alfresco.repo.web.scripts.servlet.BasicHttpAuthenticatorFactory) fetched based on the servlet init-param—authenticator (webscripts. authenticator.basic) and required server properties.

3. After completing initialization on the first request and also on subsequent requests to the /alfresco/service/* URL pattern to execute the web script, the service() method of WebScriptServlet gets invoked.

4. `WebScriptServlet` while serving the web script requests will do the following each time:

    ° It creates a new instance of web script Servlet Runtime (`org.springframework.extensions.webscripts.servlet.WebScriptServletRuntime`) using the Web Script Container, authentication factory (related classes mentioned in the second step), server properties, request (`javax.servlet.http.HttpServletRequest`), and response (`javax.servlet.http.HttpServletResponse`).

    ° It invokes the `executeScript` method of `WebScriptServletRuntime`.

5. `WebScriptServletRuntime` does not provide an implementation for the `executeScript()` method and hence the method implementation in its parent class, `AbstractRuntime` (`org.springframework.extensions.webscripts.AbstractRuntime`), gets executed.

6. During the execution of the `executeScript()` method in `AbstractRuntime`, it will first get the web script method and web script URI and invokes the `findWebscript(methodName, uri)` method of registry (`org.springframework.extensions.webscripts.DeclarativeRegistry`) defined in the Web Script Container.

7. Registry (`DeclarativeRegistry`) will perform the `uriIndex` lookup for the first request of the web script URI by invoking `findWebscript(methodName, uri)` of the `UriIndex` implementation (`org.springframework.extensions.webscripts.JaxRSUriIndex`) and update the `uriIndexCache` with the web script URI. So that in the next request for the same web script URI, the registry does not do the look up again.

8. Registry (`DeclarativeRegistry`) provides the Match object (`org.springframework.extensions.webscripts.Match`), which contains the templatePath, templateVars map, and WebScript object (`org.springframework.extensions.webscripts.DeclarativeWebScript`) back to `AbstractRuntime`.

9. Web Script Runtime (`AbstractRuntime`) then creates the WebScriptRequest (`org.springframework.extensions.webscripts.WebScriptRequestImpl`), WebScriptResponse (`org.springframework.extensions.webscripts.WebScriptResponseImpl`), and Authenticator (`org.alfresco.repo.web.scripts.servlet.BasicHttpAuthenticatorFactory.BasicHttpAuthenticator`) using the implementation available in `WebscriptServletRuntime`.

10. Web Script Runtime (`AbstractRuntime`) will then invoke the `executeScript` method of Web Script Container (`org.alfresco.repo.web.scripts.RepositoryContainer`), and pass the web script request, web script response, and authenticator. The Repository Container configured is `TenantRepositoryContainer`; however, it does not provide the implementation of the `executeScript` method and hence, the method gets executed from its parent class.

11. The Web Script Container (`RepositoryContainer`) will get the description object using the web script object received in the web script request and it first authenticates the user, creates a new transaction to execute the web script, and then invoke web script's (`DeclarativeWebScript`) execute method passing web script request and response.

12. `DeclarativeWebScript` will invoke the `getExecuteScript` method of `AbstractWebScript`, which will get the script from the web script cache. If the web script is executed for the first time, it will add it to the cache first.

13. `DeclarativeWebScript` will then invoke the `createScriptParameters` method of the `AbstractWebScript` class, which will populate a map with required parameters such as `webscript`, `format`, `args`, `argsM`, `headers`, `headersM`, `guest`, `url`, `msg`, Web Script Runtime's script parameters, and Web Script Container's script parameter. Also, it will create `TemplateConfigModel` and `ScriptConfigModel` based on `config.xml` provided for the web script.

14. In further processing, the `executeScript` method of `AbstractWebscript` will get invoked, which in turn will invoke the `ScriptProcessor` class (`org.alfresco.repo.jscript.RhinoScriptProcessor`), which will for the first time compile the JavaScript controller and resolve the imports of the script and then finally execute the controller.

15. `DeclarativeWebScript` will then have `TemplateProcessor` configured in Web Script Container (`AbstractRuntimeContainer`) to process the template in order to render the response.

16. `DeclarativeWebScript` sets the response to be rendered.

17. Web Script Container (`RepositoryContainer`) ends the transaction and resets the authentication.

18. Web Script Runtime (`AbstractRuntime`) completes the entire execution and logs the processing time of the web script execution and processing.

19. `WebscriptServlet` returns the response back to the web script client.

Components of the web script framework

The different high-level components that collectively make the powerful web script framework are as follows:

- Web Script Runtime
- Web Script Authenticator
- Web Script Container
- Other supporting components

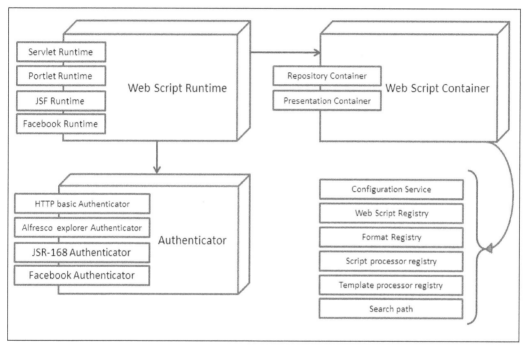

Web script framework components

Let's go through them one by one.

Web Script Runtime

Having understood the web script execution flow in detail, let's recollect the role of Web Script Runtime. While executing the web script, request dispatcher will first send the request to the Web Script Runtime. The Web Script Runtime then passes the control to the Web Script Container for further processing. Hence, it can be considered as the entry point into the web script framework after the request dispatcher.

Each and every web script gets executed in Web Script Runtime. It basically separates out the web script and its execution environment. Web Script Runtime encapsulates the complete web script execution environment, specifically requests, response, and authentication, and serves the web script to the calling web script client.

Alfresco provides different Web Script Runtimes for web script execution out-of-the-box as follows:

- Servlet Runtime
- Portlet Runtime
- JSF Runtime
- Facebook Runtime
- SURF Web Framework Runtime

Servlet Runtime

This Web Script Runtime is responsible for executing all the web scripts requested through HTTP or HTTPS requests.

 Servlet Runtime is the most commonly used runtime that basically executes web scripts using HTTP/HTTPS requests. This book also specifically focuses on Servlet Runtime.

The implementation of this runtime is available in `org.springframework.extensions.webscripts.servlet.WebScriptServletRuntime` present in `spring-webscripts-*.jar`.

Portlet Runtime

This Web Script Runtime makes it possible for JSR-168 portlets to directly execute Alfresco web scripts. Whenever Alfresco web script is accessed from the JSR-168 portlets, this runtime will get instantiated while executing the web script.

The implementation of this runtime (`PortletRuntime`) is available as an inner class implementation in `org.springframework.extensions.webscripts.portlet.WebScriptPortlet` residing in `spring-webscripts-*.jar`.

JSF Runtime

JSF components can execute Alfresco web scripts using JSF Runtime. Whenever the Alfresco web script is invoked from the JSF page, this runtime will get instantiated for executing the web script.

The implementation of this runtime (`WebScriptJSFRuntime`) can be found as an inner class implementation in `org.springframework.extensions.webscripts.jsf.UIWebScript` located in `spring-webscripts-*.jar`.

Facebook Runtime

Facebook Runtime provides access to Facebook APIs in the Alfresco web scripts.

The implementation of this runtime is available in `org.alfresco.repo.web.scripts.facebook.FacebookServletRuntime` in `alfresco-remote-api-*.jar`.

SURF Runtime

The SURF web framework runtime allows building up web-tier UI pages by embedding the Alfresco web script components.

The implementation of the SURF runtime can be found in `org.springframework.extensions.webscripts.LocalWebScriptRuntime` in `spring-surf-*.jar`.

Web Script Authenticator

When interacting with any content repository, secure access to content is a must and is really essential. Alfresco also requires an authenticated access while accessing the content repository. The main task of the Web Script Authenticator is to authenticate web script requests.

There are different authenticators, as mentioned in the following list, available out-of-the-box in Alfresco, which can be configured in the relevant Alfresco Web Script Runtime in order to provide secure access to the Alfresco repository through Alfresco web scripts:

- HTTP basic Authenticator
- Alfresco explorer Authenticator
- JSR-168 Authenticator
- JSR-168 Authenticator with Alfresco explorer support
- Facebook Authenticator

The web script framework by default uses basic HTTP authentication. However, it can be configured to use other forms of authentication mechanisms.

HTTP basic authenticator

A username and password or a ticket must be specified while accessing the web script through an HTTP/HTTPS request when web script needs to be invoked for an authenticated user.

The authorization header must contain a username and password or a ticket.

The ticket can be specified through a query string parameter: `alf_ticket`.

> A ticket basically represents an authenticated user who has already performed successful login to Alfresco. It can be easily obtained using the out-of-the-box Alfresco web script via the URL `http://localhost:8080/alfresco/service/api/login?u={username}&pw={password}`. You just need to provide the username and password in the placeholders here before invoking it. Generally, while accessing the Alfresco repository from your custom frontend application or third-party system, this would be the first thing you will do in order to proceed further and invoke other web scripts with authenticated access.

Servlet Runtime uses an HTTP basic authenticator to authenticate the web script requesting user.

This authenticator is configured as a spring bean having ID `webscripts.authenticator.basic` in `web-scripts-application-context.xml`.

> The `web-scripts-application-context.xml` file can be located at `tomcat\webapps\alfresco\WEB-INF\classes\alfresco` inside your Alfresco installed directory. If you are using Alfresco Community 5, it can be located under the `alfresco` package inside `alfresco-remote-api-*.jar`.

Alfresco explorer authenticator

This authenticator uses the authentication mechanism that is used while logging to Alfresco Web Client.

The user will be redirected to the Alfresco Web Client login page if a login is required.

This authenticator is configured as a spring bean having ID `webscripts.authenticator.webclient` in `web-client-application-context.xml`.

The web-client-application-context.xml file can be found at tomcat\webapps\alfresco\WEB-INF\classes\ alfresco inside your Alfresco installed directory. The location remains the same for Alfresco Community 5 as well.

JSR-168 Authenticator

JSR-168 Authenticator expects the user has been already authenticated by the portal. Authenticated portal user can be found from the portal session using the alfportletusername attribute.

This authenticator is configured as a spring bean having ID webscripts. authenticator.jsr168 in web-scripts-application-context.xml.

JSR-168 Authenticator with Alfresco Explorer support

Alfresco repository web scripts, depending on Alfresco Web Client functionalities, can be authenticated and used within the portal with the use of this authenticator.

This authenticator is configured as a spring bean having ID webscripts. authenticator.jsr168.webclient in web-client-application-context.xml.

Facebook Authenticator

Users will be redirected to the Facebook login page if a login is required.

This authenticator is configured as a spring bean having ID as webscripts. authenticator.facebook in web-scripts-application-context.xml.

Web Script Container

Web Script Container is the core of the web script framework. It plays a major role in executing the web script by being a central point integrating all other required services in order to execute web script. It identifies the appropriate web script and provides the root objects to the web script.

Alfresco out-of-the-box provides two types of Web Script Containers:

- Repository Container
- Presentation Container

Repository Container

This container plays a key role in executing all the web scripts that provide direct access to the content residing in the Alfresco repository using the various services provided by Alfresco.

It is a specialized type of container mainly to be embedded only in the Alfresco repository. It uses some of the core services provided by the Alfresco repository to support transactions and authentication for web scripts.

Another useful and important thing that the Repository Container does is that it provides the repository-specific root objects available for the JavaScript based-controller and response templates.

Repository Container configuration can be found in Alfresco's web app in `web-scripts-application-context.xml` as a bean entry having ID `webscripts.container`.

In the recent versions of Alfresco (Version 4 onwards), implementation class is `org.alfresco.repo.web.scripts.TenantRepositoryContainer,` found in `alfresco-remote-api-*.jar.`

Presentation Container

Presentation Container is a lightweight implementation mainly for web scripts to render user interface components making remote calls to remote repositories. It provides the basic support to web scripts for making service call to remote data sources.

This is available as the vanilla container in the spring web scripts implementation that gets shipped with Alfresco. This container implementation makes it easy to host web scripts in any environment.

Presentation Container configuration can be found in `spring-webscripts-*.jar` as a spring bean entry having ID `webscripts.container` in `web-scripts-application-context.xml.`

Other supporting components

The various other components that Web Script Container relies upon and which play a key role while the execution of web scripts are being executed are explored in the following sections.

Configuration service

All relevant XML configuration files for the web script are read and parsed using the configuration service.

The implementation class is `org.springframework.extensions.config.xml.XMLConfigService`.

Web Script registry

Indexes for all the web scripts that are registered to the specific Web Script Container are maintained using the web script registry.

The implementation class is `org.springframework.extensions.webscripts.DeclarativeRegistry`.

Format registry

Format registry is the registry to get the relevant format for the specified MIME type and also to get the MIME type for the mentioned format.

The `org.springframework.extensions.webscripts.FormatRegistry` class contains the implementation details.

Script processor registry

The script processor registry provides a script processor that executes the backend implementation of the web script controller implemented in JavaScript.

The implementation of the script processor registry can be found in `org.springframework.extensions.webscripts.ScriptProcessorRegistry`.

The script processor used to execute the JavaScript-based controller is `org.alfresco.repo.jscript.RhinoScriptProcessor`.

Template processor registry

The template processor registry provides the template processor that executes the response templates for the web script.

The implementation of it can be located in `org.springframework.extensions.webscripts.TemplateProcessorRegistry`.

The Default FreeMarker template processor implementation is available in `org.springframework.extensions.webscripts.processor.FTLTemplateProcessor`.

Search path

The search path contains the list of stores and is basically an endpoint location for web script files. This is useful while doing the lookup for web script files.

The implementation for it can be found at `org.springframework.extensions.webscripts.SearchPath`.

Understanding the wiring of web script framework components

All of the web script framework components we have gone through work together through Spring configuration. Let's take a look at the core configuration files that wire up the web script framework components together as a part of web script framework in Alfresco:

- The vanilla implementation for spring-related configurations for the web script framework is available in `spring-webscripts-application-context.xml` in `spring-webscripts-*.jar`.

- An extended version of the web script framework-related spring configuration to support Alfresco repository embedding can be found in the Alfresco web app in `web-scripts-application-context.xml` at the location mentioned earlier.

Deployment architecture

Web script framework is designed in such a way that it can be hosted in different environments not limited to just the Alfresco repository server.

Web Script Runtime plays a key role in providing encapsulation of execution environment of the web script and provides different implementations to execute web scripts. The most common way to access the web script is through HTTP/HTTPS requests and Servlet Runtime is the most commonly used Web Script Runtime that is responsible for executing web scripts accessed through HTTP requests.

Web Script Runtime makes it easy to execute RESTful Alfresco web scripts in various ways such as execution in JSF components, portlets using their own way to invoke the Alfresco web scripts.

The typical deployment architecture would be to have all the data web scripts hosted in the Alfresco repository server. The frontend clients using the backend repository can use presentation web scripts to build up the frontend user interface and presentation web scripts will be hosted at the client side. Frontend clients can invoke data web scripts through HTTP in order to interact with the backend repository. The Alfresco repository server will use Servlet Runtime to execute the web scripts.

Summary

In this chapter, we learned the web script execution flow in detail along with its technical details. Also, we went through the different components that collectively make up the web script framework. We have also gone through the various out-of-the-box implementations available in Alfresco for these components and the most common deployment architecture of Alfresco web scripts.

As we have explored the web script framework in Alfresco, we are going to take a look at the various components in detail for building up web script in the next chapter.

4
Building Blocks of Web Scripts

In this chapter, we will cover different components in detail to create a web script:

- The description document
- Controller implementation
- Response templates
- I18N message bundle
- The configuration document
- Naming conventions for each component

Web scripts is a key feature of the Alfresco enterprise content management system and it's easy to implement. Having detailed knowledge about the components that make a web script will make your job even easier to develop web scripts in Alfresco.

This chapter will provide you with the detailed knowledge about the building blocks of web scripts. It is really essential to have thorough understanding about the different artifacts that are used to develop web scripts in Alfresco. Throughout your journey of Alfresco web scripts implementation in any of your project, you will always have to use these components while developing web scripts, and hence, it is very important to get a clear understanding of it so that you can quickly and easily implement web scripts whenever required.

Alfresco provides a powerful web script framework that makes it easy to create a web script using familiar technologies such as scripting and template languages. Each and every web script must have a description document and have at least one or more FreeMarker response template document. Web scripts can optionally have a controller as a backend implementation that will do the required processing against Alfresco repository as per the defined business logic. There are some optional advanced implementations also possible to have message bundle for web script responses along with some configuration options for web scripts if required.

Let's take a look at each of the components of web script in detail to gain better understanding of them.

The description document – it's a must!

While developing web scripts, the first thing to do is perform a brief exercise to decide on the URI and HTTP method of the web script, any arguments to be provided to the web script, the response format to be used for the web script, check whether any authentication is to be used for the web script or not, and check whether any backend processing is required with the repository or not, and then start with the implementation and first create the description document for the web script.

A description document is the core of web script implementation, and it is basically an XML file. It describes the important details about a web script. Any developer taking a look at the description document can get an idea about what the web script does at a high level.

This is the first file that needs to be developed while creating a web script in Alfresco. There are certain mandatory declarations that must be provided in the web script description document for a web script. Apart from this, there are additional declarations that can optionally be provided for a web script. Let's now take a look at the various declarations that can be provided in the description document. We will take a look at the options one by one, which will give you a clear understanding about how to create a description document, `helloworld.get.desc.xml`, from scratch for the hello world web script we created earlier.

Mandatory declarations

Now let's go through the elements that must be provided in the description document while creating a web script.

The <webscript> tag

All the information about a web script is captured in the web script description document within the root element, `<webscript>`:

```
<webscript>
</webscript>
```

If you do not specify the preceding root element tag and create a blank description document XML file, then while registering the web script, an error will appear in the log and you will not be able to register the web script.

The following is the snippet of the error from the logs:

Unable to register script workspace://SpacesStore/app:company_home/ app:dictionary/cm:extensionwebscripts/helloworld.get.desc.xml due to error: Failed to parse web script description document helloworld.get.desc.xml; Error on line -1 of document: Premature end of file. Nested exception: Premature end of file.

The <shortname> tag

For any web scripts, a human-readable name of the web script is always given. It can be provided within the `<shortname>` tag as seen in the following code line. This tag does not have any attributes.

```
<shortname>Hello World</shortname>
```

If you try to register the web script without providing the `shortname` value, it will not get registered. The following is the snippet of the error that will appear in the logs:

Unable to register script workspace://SpacesStore/app:company_home/ app:dictionary/cm:extensionwebscripts/helloworld.get.desc.xml due to error: Failed to parse web script description document helloworld.get.desc.xml; Expected <shortname> value.

The <url> tag

Each web script is bound to a URI that will be used to invoke the web script. It is possible to have one or more URI declaration for a web script, and any of the URIs can be used to execute the web scripts. This tag does not have any attributes:

```
<url>/helloworld?name={argumentName}</url>
<url>/hello/world/{argumentName}</url>
```

If a URL is not provided in the description document and you try to register the web script, it will give an error and will not register the web script. The following is the snippet of the error from the logs when there isn't any URL provided in the web script description document:

Unable to register script workspace://SpacesStore/app:company_home/ app:dictionary/cm:extensionwebscripts/helloworld.get.desc.xml due to error: Failed to parse web script description document helloworld.get.desc.xml; Expected at least one <url> element.

If a URL has been defined in one web script and you try to define the same URL in another web script, then the web script engine will not register the web script and an error as shown in the following example will appear in the logs:

Unable to register script classpath:alfresco/extension/templates/webscripts/test/ helloworld1.get.desc.xml due to error: Web Script document test/helloworld1.get. desc.xml is attempting to define the url '/helloworld1:GET' already defined by test/ helloworld.get.desc.xml.

A minimal description file with all the mandatory elements for a hello world web script will appear as follows:

```
<webscript>
  <shortname>Hello World</shortname>
  <url>/helloworld?name={argumentName}</url>
  <url>/hello/world/{argumentName}</url>
</webscript>
```

Optional declarations

Along with mandatory declarations, it is also possible to have some additional elements declared in the description document. Let's take a walk-through of the possible optional declarations for the web script description document.

<format>

This element allows you to specify the response content type through the web script URI while invoking the web scripts. It basically allows you to control how to specify the web script response format. There are different possible valid values that can be defined for this element and are mentioned in the subsequent sections. This element has an optional attribute named `default`.

argument

Let's take a look at the `format` tag that has its value as `argument` in the description document. It will appear as follows:

```
<format default="html">argument</format>
```

Specifying the value `argument` for the `format` element indicates that the response format for a web script can be selected by adding an argument to the web script URL. Using the query string parameter `format`, the response content type can be specified as follows:

```
http://localhost:8080/alfresco/service/helloworld?name=Ramesh&format=
xml
```

extension

The `format` tag that has its value as `extension` will appear in the description document as follows:

```
<format default="html">extension</format>
```

It is possible to specify the response content-type by adding an extension to the web script ID while invoking the web script as follows:

```
http://localhost:8080/alfresco/service/helloworld.xml?name=Ramesh
```

any

In the description document, when `any` is specified as a value for the `format` tag, the response format can be specified using any of the previous methods mentioned. In a scenario where there is no `format` element specified in the description document, it would be considered the same as having the `format` value specified as `any`. The `format` tag that has its value as `any` will appear in the description document as follows:

```
<format default="html">any</format>
```

 When the response content type is not specified at all while invoking the web script, the `default` content type is taken using the `default` attribute of the `format` tag. If the default attribute is not set, then its default value is HTML. It is also possible for some web scripts to decide on the response content type at runtime. For them, specify the `default` attribute as blank, for example, `default=""`.

<authentication>

In order to securely access the web scripts, it is important to specify the level of authentication required for the web script. It can be defined using this optional tag declaration. It has an optional attribute: `runas`. The different possible values that can be specified for this element are explained in the subsequent sections.

none

If you want to implement a web script that does not require authentication, you can specify the `authentication` tag in the description document of a web script as follows:

```
<authentication>none</authentication>
```

This is the default value when the `authentication` tag is also not specified in the description document. It indicates that there isn't any authentication required to run the web script.

 In a web script that has authentication specified as none, it will not be possible to interact with the repository.

guest

You can specify the `authentication` tag using `guest` value as follows:

```
<authentication>guest</authentication>
```

The previous line indicates that to run the web script, guest level authentication is required at the minimum.

user

You can specify the `authentication` tag that has its value as `user` as follows:

```
<authentication>user</authentication>
```

This specifies that repository's named user authentication is required at the minimum to run the web script.

admin

You can specify the `authentication` tag that has its value as `admin` as follows:

```
<authentication>admin</authentication>
```

The previous line indicates that a repository's admin user authentication is required to run the web script. An admin user is basically a user that belongs to the `ALFRESCO_ADMINISTRATORS` group.

It is also possible to specify to execute the web script as a specific Alfresco repository user irrespective of who initiated the web script. This can be specified using the `runas` attribute of authentication element, for example, `runas="admin"`.

It is important to note that this attribute is only available for the web scripts placed in the Java classpath.

<transaction>

It is also possible to specify the transaction level in order to execute the web script using this optional `transaction` element. This element has two optional attributes: `allow` and `buffersize`. The different possible valid values for this element are as in the subsequent sections:

none

The `transaction` that has its value as `none` will appear in the description document as follows:

```
<transaction>none</transaction>
```

The previous line indicates that in order to run the web script, no transaction is required.

required

The `transaction` tag that has its value as `required` will appear as follows:

```
<transaction>required</transaction>
```

The previous line specifies that a transaction is required in order to run the web script. Existing transaction, if available, will be used to execute the web script; otherwise, a new transaction will be created in order to execute the web script.

requiresnew

The `transaction` tag that has its value as `requiresnew` will appear as follows:

```
<transaction>requiresnew</transaction>
```

The previous line indicates that a new transaction is to be always created to run the web script.

 When the authentication value is set to none and the transaction element is not provided in the description document, the default value for transaction is none.

When the authentication value is not none, the default value for transaction is `required`.

The `allow` attribute will specify the type of allowed data transfer. Valid values are `readonly` (indicates the read-only transfer) and `readwrite` (indicates the read-write transfer).

Another attribute, `buffersize`, specifies an integer value that represents the size of buffer in bytes. This is the size the web script will allocate to guard against the rollback of transaction during processing. In a scenario of rollback, if the buffer is not full, then it can simply rollback without committing the output of the web script to the container stream. Hence, it helps to return the error responses without returning the partial response from the web script that has errors added to it.

<family>

The `family` tag is used in order to categorize the web scripts. Similar types of web scripts can be classified to be of the same family by specifying the same value in the `family` tag in the description document for them. It is possible to have multiple entries of this tag in the description document if a web script can be categorized to belong to a different family. The `family` tag in the description document will appear as follows:

```
<family>name of family</family>
```

An example of the `family` tag is as follows:

```
<family>CMIS</family>
```

When you access the `http://localhost:8080/alfresco/service/index` page, you should find an option to browse the web scripts based on family. For example, you will find a link **Browse 'CMIS' Web Scripts** to take a look at all the web scripts categorized to be of the CMIS family.

<cache>

Caching is a very good feature that helps to avoid regenerating a response for each request. The web script framework in Alfresco uses the caching mechanism defined by HTTP. For a web script, the required level of caching can be provided using this optional element. When a web script is invoked, the web script framework translates the declaration of this element to an appropriate response header to manage the cache. The `cache` tag with its child elements will appear in the description document as follows:.

```
<cache>
    <never>false</never>
    <public>true</public>
    <mustrevalidate/>
</cache>
```

The different optional child elements of this tag are explained in the subsequent sections.

never

This indicates whether a web script response should be cached or not. The default value is `true`, which means that a web script response will never be cached. An alternate value is `false` to specify allowing of caching of a web script response.

public

This is used to specify whether the authenticated web script response should be cached in a public cache or not. The `true` value indicates that the web script response can be cached, while `false` indicates the web script response can not be cached. The default value is `false`.

mustrevalidate

This is used to indicate whether a cache should revalidate its version of the web script response in order to provide the fresh response data. The `true` value indicates that there must always be a validation, while `false` indicates there might be a validation. The default value is always `true`.

<negotiate>

For the specific web script response format, the `accept` header MIME type can be provided using this optional element. There can be multiple entries of this element in the description document. It is mandatory to provide the value for this tag. The value will hold the type of response format. Also, it is mandatory to provide the `accept` attribute that mentions the MIME type.

```
<negotiate accept="text/html">html</negotiate>
<negotiate accept="text/xml">xml</negotiate>
```

With the definition of one `negotiate` element in the description document, content negotiation is enabled.

> It is interesting to understand how the `negotiate` and `format` elements are correlated. Each web script returns result in a response stream and it might be encoded based on the MIME type. If during invoking a web script, any hint is not provided on the MIME type, then the web script framework will use its predefined encoding. While invoking a web script, it is possible to provide the hint to let the web script framework know about the MIME type for response. Using the `format` element, as a URL extension or as a format argument, the response format can be specified, which is mapped to a MIME type in the web script framework. Another option is to specify the `Accept` header, which can be done using the negotiate element.

<lifecycle>

The lifecycle element is to describe the lifecycle stage of a web script. This element can be specified in the description document as follows:

```
<lifecycle>sample</lifecycle>
```

Web scripts in their development lifecycle can initially be in draft state, then are fully used in the production mode, and at the end are deprecated when they are not used anymore. These stages can be specified for web scripts using this element. Different possible values for this element are shown in the subsequent sections.

none

This indicates that the web script is not part of any lifecycle.

sample

This mentions that the web script is a sample web script and should not be used for production use.

draft

This specifies that the web script is still in the experimental stage and not yet fully completed.

public_api

This determines that the web script is part of the Alfresco public API, and hence, it is fully tested and must be stable.

draft_public_api

This mentions that it is going to be a part of the Alfresco public API but it is not yet fully complete or still some changes are in progress.

deprecated

This indicates the web script is deprecated and should not be used and that this web script may be removed from the future Alfresco versions.

internal

This mentions that the web script is for Alfresco internal use only. Hence, for different versions, it could have been changed as per the Alfresco internal usage, and it's a possibility that it can be changed in future versions of Alfresco.

 The `<lifecycle>` element is an optional one. Generally, for the custom web scripts that you will develop for your project, it is not mandatory to specify the `lifecycle` value for a web script. Hence, you might not be using this element.

<formdata>

In the description document of a web script, you can specify the `formdata` tag as follows:

```
<formdata multipart-processing="false" />
```

It has an attribute called `multipart-processing`. This can be used to specify whether multipart form data processing is turned on or off for the web script. Optional values are `true`, which indicates that multipart processing for form data is turned on and `false`, which indicates that it is off. The default value is `true`.

<args>

The `args` element is used generally for documentation purposes to describe the arguments passed to the web script. It has the child element `arg`, which has child elements `name`, which specifies the name of the argument, and `description`, which specifies a description of the argument. The `args` tag with its child element will appear in the description document as follows:

```
<args>
  <arg>
    <name>name</name>
    <description>the name to display for helloworld
      webscript</description>
  </arg>
</args>
```

<requests>

The `requests` element can be used to specify the collection of request types. It has `request` as a child element, which has `type` as an attribute. This tag will appear in the description document as follows:

```
<requests>
  <request type="cmis.atomentry "/>
</requests>
```

<responses>

The `responses` element can be used to specify the collection of response types. It has `response` as a child element, which has `type` as the attribute. This tag will appear in the description document as follows:

```
<responses>
    <response type="cmis.atomentry"/>
</responses>
```

kind

The `kind` attribute is an optional attribute to the root tag `<webscript>`. A special kind of implementation can be done for web scripts, which is basically a Java backend implementation. For example, in a scenario where you want to develop web scripts that need to return large content as the response, a Java-backed web script implementation can be developed for this scenario. The `kind` attribute allows you to provide a name for this implementation. Now, for any web script you are developing that has to render large amount of content, the `kind` attribute can be used in the description document to explicitly mention that it should use the custom Java backend implementation created.

Here is an example of how the `kind` attribute is used in the out-of-the-box Alfresco web script, `tomcat/webapps/alfresco/WEB-INF/classes/alfresco/templates/webscripts/org/alfresco/repository/thumbnail/thumbnail.get.desc.xml`, inside your Alfresco installation directory. If you are using Alfresco Community 5, the `thumbnail.get.desc.xml` file can be located under the `alfresco` package in `alfresco-remote-api-*.jar`.

```
<webscript kind="org.alfresco.repository.content.stream">
```

Controller implementation – not mandatory!

The actual business logic for a web script resides in the web script controller. The main functionalities such as interacting with repository, for example, to query the repository, add content, update content, delete content, and so on are part of the web script controller implementation.

There are two types of controller implementations possible to implement while creating web scripts in Alfresco:

- The JavaScript-backed controller
- The Java-backed controller

The JavaScript-backed controller

JavaScript-backed controller is known as the web script controller script that has the web script business logic implemented in a JavaScript file. Alfresco provides a set of JavaScript APIs that can be used in the web script controller to interact with the Alfresco backend repository. A JavaScript controller can read the query string parameters of the web script URI, perform the required repository operations, and populate the model object to render the response.

We have already seen the basic implementation of JavaScript controller for our hello world web script.

Understanding when to use the JavaScript controller

Here are a few generic points that explain when you should go for JavaScript controller implementation for your web script:

- When the repository operations you are trying to perform can be easily done using the available Alfresco JavaScript API, you might choose this controller

- The JavaScript controller has an advantage that if you have developed a web script that has a controller using the JavaScript implementation, you do not need to restart the server to deploy and use your web script

- No additional tooling is required; you can simply use any editor to create the web script, no compilation is required, and is easy to deploy in the repository

The Java-backed controller

The Java-backed controller is another type of controller implementation possible to implement for a web script that might have the complete business logic processing implemented in Java.

When you are implementing a Java-backed controller, you will have access to all the content application services available in Alfresco. Business logic implementation for a web script can be provided in JavaScript- or Java-based controller; the only difference is that Java-backed controller is implemented in Java and it has access to all the available content application services in Alfresco.

Understanding when to use a Java-backed controller

Let's take a look at a few points about when you should go for the Java-backed controller implementation for your web script:

- Generally, when the JavaScript controller cannot do the repository operations you want to do using the available Alfresco JavaScript API, you should implement the Java-backed controller.

- When you want to override the rendering of a response, for example, rendering large content in response, you should use this controller.

- Consider that you will require experience in Java programming. You will also require compilation of the Java code, classpath deployment of web scripts, and even server restart in order to use Java-backed web script. If all of this looks fine to achieve your business functionality in time, then you can go for implementing Java-backed controller.

 A web script can also have both JavaScript- and Java-backed controllers. In such a scenario, the Java-backed controller will first get executed and then JavaScript-based implementation gets executed when the web script is invoked.

Response templates – yes, they are required!

Response templates are basically used to render the web script response. In MVC terms, response templates play a role of views. The output of the web script is rendered in the required formats using the web script response templates.

It is possible to have multiple response templates for a web script, and based on the requested response content type while invoking a web script, a response can be rendered using the appropriate response template.

Response template also has access to web script query string parameters along with the data items provided by the controller script and access to some common content repository entry points.

We have already seen rendering response for our hello world web script.

 For JavaScript-based web scripts, response templates are always required. There are certain implementations of Java-backed web scripts where response can be directly rendered from the Java controller. In such case, there is no need to specify response template for the web script. We are going to cover Java-backed web scripts in detail in *Chapter 6, Creating Java-backed Web Scripts*.

I18N for a web script – it's optional

Internationalization is a cool feature that can be very useful while creating web scripts.

There may be times when you are required to develop a web script that will directly be used by the end users, and hence, you need a human-readable web script response in the user's language. No worries, it is possible to provide I18N support to the web scripts in Alfresco, and hence, you can have the text in the response rendered in the preferred supported user languages.

We will also extend our hello world web script to have internationalization support and will get understanding of how to make a web script render a response using internationalization.

There are two things to be done in order to achieve this:

- Creating a resource bundle for different languages
- Modifying the response template to use the labels from the resource bundle

Adding a resource bundle for the hello world web script

In order to add a resource bundle for a web script, the first thing we need to do is create a resource bundle for the different languages.

After logging in to Alfresco Share, create `helloworld.get.properties` at the **Repository | Data Dictionary | Web Scripts Extensions** location, and add the following content to it:

```
greeting.title=Hello!
email.title=email address
```

Now, at the same location, create `helloworld.get_de.properties` and add the following content to it:

```
greeting.title=Hallo!
email.title=E-Mail-Adresse
```

We have just created two properties files and made the text able to be rendered in the web script response in two different languages: English and German.

Modifying the response template to use labels

Now, in order to use the labels added in the resource bundle, we will have to modify the response template. Perform the following steps to modify the response template for the hello world web script:

1. Modify `helloworld.get.html.ftl` available at the **Repository | Data Dictionary | Web Scripts Extensions** location as follows:

```
<html>
  <body>
    <p>${msg("greeting.title")}${args.name}.</p>
    <p>${msg("email.title")}: ${email}</p>
  </body>
</html>
```

We have just modified our response template to use the text from the resource bundle.

2. Now, go to `http://localhost:8080/alfresco/service/index` and click on the **Refresh Web Scripts** button.

3. To test this, temporarily change the preferred browser language to Germany de-DE and hit the `http://localhost:8080/alfresco/service/helloworld?name=Ramesh` URL. You should see the response rendered using the labels rendered from German properties file we created.

Configuration document – it's optional

It is possible to specify configuration parameters for Alfresco web scripts. They can be accessed from the controller as well as the response template. Just to understand the concept, let's take a simple example where you want to display the server environment (development, testing, staging, or production server) in your web script output. One thing that you can do is specify the same in controller, but ideally, a controller should not worry about such configurations. Instead, this can be handled separately and the controller or template should just use the values. With the web script configuration document, it is possible to do script specific configuration.

Create `helloworld.get.config.xml` at the **Repository** | **Data Dictionary** | **Web Scripts Extensions** location and add the following content to it:

```
<properties>
   <envname>Dev</envname>
</properties>
```

Accessing configuration in a controller

In the JavaScript controller, the `envname` property can be accessible as follows:

```
var env = new XML(config.script);
logger.log(env.envname);
```

You can set the value of `envname` property in the model object and render the value on the response template.

Accessing configuration in a template

In a scenario when no controller implementation is available for the web script, the `envname` property can be accessed directly in the response FreeMarker template as follows:

```
${config.script["properties"]["envname"]}
```

We have seen two different ways to display value from the web script configuration. I am sure you can now easily test them in the hello world web script and see the result.

Naming conventions – the most important thing

It is important to follow the naming conventions for the web script documents. The following are the naming conventions that must be followed for each web script document:

Component	Naming convention
Description document	`<web script id>.<http method>.desc.xml`
Controller script	`<web script id>.<http method>.js`
Response template	`<web script id>.<http method>.<extension>.ftl`
Configuration document	`<web script id>.<http method>.config.xml`
Resource bundle	`<web script id>.<http method>[_<locale>].properties` Locale is basically a combination of the language code and country code, for example, en_US, where en is the language code and US is the country code.

The `<web script id>` is the identifier of the web script, and must be a unique value in the web script package. For example, you can have `helloworld.get.desc.xml` in two different web script packages, which is basically a way to categorize web script, and must have different URIs.

Summary

In this chapter, we gained knowledge about the different components (both mandatory and optional) in detail to develop web scripts in Alfresco. We gained a better understanding about description document that is the core of any web script, possible controller implementation, response templates, the configuration document for a web script, and internationalization of a web script, as well as the important naming conventions to follow for the web script implementation for each of these documents. Overall, you have now got the required understanding of the web script building blocks.

In the next chapter, we are going to take a look at the different ways to invoke the web scripts.

5
Invoking Web Scripts

In this chapter, we will cover how to invoke an Alfresco web script in different ways such as the following:

- Invoking a web script through web browser and REST client plugins
- Executing a web script through a standalone Java program
- Making a call to a web script from Spring-based services
- Different ways to invoke a web script from Alfresco Share
- Calling a web script from the command line
- Calling a web script from JSF pages or JSR-168 portals
- Dealing with the limitation of clients

While working with web scripts in Alfresco, there might be situations where you would be curious to know how to execute a web script. For example, some common practical scenarios such as while developing web scripts, you will be interested in unit testing it. You want to invoke the web script in order to verify that the web script works well and returns the output as expected. In a support project while working on custom frontend application with a backend Alfresco repository, in the process of fixing an issue during debugging, you need to execute the web script and verify the response in order to find out whether the issue was a frontend issue or a backend issue. While working on customizing Alfresco Share, you will need to call the Alfresco repository web script. Sometimes, you might be required to make a call to the web script from a standalone Java class. It might be possible that you have a Spring-based application and from there you want to invoke an Alfresco web script. At some point of time, you might be required to call a web script from a Linux shell script as well and the list of such scenarios goes on.

It is useful to have an understanding of how to invoke a web script in such basic possible real-life implementation scenarios. In this chapter, we are going to take a look at how to invoke web scripts in the previously mentioned common scenarios that any developer at some point of time will come across while working with Alfresco.

Invoking a web script from a web browser

One of the easiest ways to invoke a web script is through a web browser. This is a convenient option for everyone. A web browser is a common client everyone generally uses to invoke a web script to test it while developing web scripts.

Every HTTP GET web script you develop can simply be executed from a web browser by just hitting the web script URL. If any authentication is required for the web script, then an authentication pop up will appear to provide the authentication details.

Executing a web script using web browser plugins

To test the web scripts you have created for POST, PUT, or DELETE, you cannot simply execute them from the web browser. You will be required to execute them through the add-ons provided by the browser to invoke HTTP POST, PUT, or DELETE calls. There could be multiple options available for browser plugins. We will take a look at two plugins here.

Poster – Firefox add-on

One plugin option is a Firefox add-on named Poster. You can download this plugin from the Firefox add-ons link, `https://addons.mozilla.org/`. If you already have Firefox installed, then open Firefox browser and just go to the add-ons link and search for `Poster`, and from the list of add-ons displayed, add **Poster** to Firefox. Another faster and easier way to install Poster is to go to **Tools** | **Add-ons** and search for `Poster` and click on the **Install** button.

Once the add-on is installed, go to **Tools** | **Poster** to open the poster window. From this window, you can provide the web script URL, authentication credentials, request headers, parameters, and specify the HTTP method to invoke the web script.

Advanced REST client for Chrome

Another good plugin option to use is the advanced REST client extension for Chrome. This plugin can be downloaded from the Chrome webstore link, `https://chrome.google.com/webstore/category/apps`. If you have already installed Chrome, then open the Chrome browser and just go to the link we just mentioned and search for `advanced rest client` and from the list of results displayed, install the **Advanced REST client** by following the Chrome extension install process. Another faster and easier way to install advanced REST client extension is to go to **Tools** | **Extension** and click on the **Get more extensions** link. Now, search for `Advanced REST client` and from the list of results displayed, install the plugin by following the Chrome extension install process.

Once the Advanced REST client plugin is installed, to invoke it, put `chrome-extension://hgmloofddffdnphfgcellkdfbfbjeloo/RestClient.html` in the address bar of your Chrome browser. Another quick and easier way to launch the advanced REST client is to enter `chrome://apps` in the address bar and hit it. You can see the advanced REST client displayed here. Just click on it. You can now execute all your web scripts of GET, POST, PUT, and DELETE methods through the Advanced REST client plugin for Chrome.

Executing a web script from standalone Java program

There are different options to invoke a web script from a Java program. Here, we will take a detailed walkthrough of the Apache commons HttpClient API with code snippets to understand how a web script can be executed from the Java program, and will briefly mention some other alternatives that can also be used to invoke web scripts from Java programs.

HttpClient

One way of executing a web script is to invoke web scripts using `org.apache.`
`commons.httpclient.HttpClient` API. This class is available in `commons-`
`httpclient-3.1.jar`. Executing a web script with HttpClient API also requires
`commons-logging-*.jar` and `commons-codec-*.jar` as supporting JARs. These
JARs are available at the `tomcat\webapps\alfresco\WEB-INF\lib` location inside
your Alfresco installation directory. You will need to include them in the build
path for your project. We will try to execute the hello world web script using the
HttpClient from a standalone Java program. While using HttpClient, here are the
steps in general you need to follow:

1. Create a new instance of HttpClient.
2. The next step is to create an instance of method (we will use `GetMethod`).
    The URL needs to be passed in the constructor of the method.
3. Set any arguments if required.
4. Provide the authentication details if required.
5. Ask HttpClient to now execute the method.
6. Read the response status code and response.
7. Finally, release the connection.

Understanding how to invoke a web script using HttpClient

Let's take a look at the following code snippet considering the previous mentioned
steps. In order to test this, you can create a standalone Java program with a main
method and put the following code snippet in Java program and then modify the
web script URLs/credentials as required. Comments are provided in the following
code snippet for you to easily correlate the previous steps with the code:

```
// Create a new instance of HttpClient
HttpClient objHttpClient = new HttpClient();

// Create a new method instance as required. Here it is GetMethod.
GetMethod objGetMethod = new GetMethod("http://localhost:8080/
alfresco/service/helloworld");

// Set querystring parameters if required.
objGetMethod.setQueryString(new NameValuePair[] { new
NameValuePair("name", "Ramesh") });

// set the credentials if authentication is required.
```

```
Credentials defaultcreds = new UsernamePasswordCredentials("admin","a
dmin");
objHttpClient.getState().setCredentials(new
AuthScope("localhost",8080, AuthScope.ANY_REALM), defaultcreds);

try {
  // Now, execute the method using HttpClient.
  int statusCode = objHttpClient.executeMethod(objGetMethod);
  if (statusCode != HttpStatus.SC_OK) {
    System.err.println("Method invocation failed: " +
      objGetMethod.getStatusLine());
  }

  // Read the response body.
  byte[] responseBody = objGetMethod.getResponseBody();

  // Print the response body.
  System.out.println(new String(responseBody));

} catch (HttpException e) {
  System.err.println("Http exception: " + e.getMessage());
  e.printStackTrace();
} catch (IOException e) {
  System.err.println("IO exception transport error: " +
    e.getMessage());
  e.printStackTrace();
} finally {
  // Release the method connection.
  objGetMethod.releaseConnection();
}
```

Note that the Apache commons client is a legacy project now and is not being developed anymore. This project has been replaced by the Apache HttpComponents project in HttpClient and HttpCore modules. We have used HttpClient from Apache commons client here to get an overall understanding.

Some of the other options that you can use to invoke web scripts from a Java program are mentioned in subsequent sections.

URLConnection

One option to execute web script from Java program is by using `java.net.URLConnection`. For more details, you can refer to `http://docs.oracle.com/javase/tutorial/networking/urls/readingWriting.html`.

Apache HTTP components

Another option to execute web script from Java program is to use Apache HTTP components that are the latest available APIs for HTTP communication. These components offer better performance and more flexibility and are available in `httpclient-*.jar` and `httpcore-*.jar`. These JARs are available at the `tomcat\webapps\alfresco\WEBINF\lib` location inside your Alfresco installation directory. For more details, refer to `https://hc.apache.org/httpcomponents-client-4.3.x/quickstart.html` to get an understanding of how to execute HTTP calls from a Java program.

RestTemplate

Another alternative would be to use `org.springframework.web.client.RestTemplate` available in `org.springframework.web-*.jar` located at `tomcat\webapps\alfresco\WEB-INF\lib` inside your Alfresco installation directory. If you are using Alfresco Community 5, the `RestTemplate` class is available in `spring-web-*.jar`. Generally, `RestTemplate` is used in Spring-based services to invoke an HTTP communication.

Calling web scripts from Spring-based services

If you need to invoke an Alfresco web script from Spring-based services, then you need to use `RestTemplate` to invoke HTTP calls. This is the most commonly used technique to execute HTTP calls from Spring-based classes. In order to do this, the following are the steps to be performed. The code snippets are also provided:

1. Define `RestTemplate` in your Spring context file:

   ```
   <bean id="restTemplate" class="org.springframework.web.client.
   RestTemplate" />
   ```

2. In the Spring context file, inject `restTemplate` in your Spring class as shown in the following example:

   ```
   <bean id="httpCommService" class="com.test.HTTPCallService">
     <property name="restTemplate" value="restTemplate" />
   </bean>
   ```

3. In the Java class, define the setter method for `restTemplate` as follows:

```
private RestTemplate restTemplate;
public void setRestTemplate(RestTemplate restTemplate) {
    this.restTemplate = restTemplate;
}
```

4. In order to invoke a web script that has an authentication level set as user authentication, you can use `RestTemplate` in your Java class as shown in the following code snippet. The following code snippet is an example to invoke the hello world web script using `RestTemplate` from a Spring-based service:

```
// setup authentication
String plainCredentials = "admin:admin";
byte[] plainCredBytes = plainCredentials.getBytes();
byte[] base64CredBytes = Base64.encodeBase64(plainCredBytes);
String base64Credentials = new String(base64CredBytes);

// setup request headers
HttpHeaders reqHeaders = new HttpHeaders();
reqHeaders.add("Authorization", "Basic " + base64Credentials);
HttpEntity<String> requestEntity = new
HttpEntity<String>(reqHeaders);

// Execute method
ResponseEntity<String> responseEntity = restTemplate.
exchange("http://localhost:8080/alfresco/service/
helloworld?name=Ramesh", HttpMethod.GET, requestEntity, String.
class);
System.out.println("Response:"+responseEntity.getBody());
```

Invoking a web script from Alfresco Share

When working on customizing Alfresco Share, you will need to make a call to Alfresco repository web scripts. In Alfresco Share, you can invoke repository web scripts from two places. One is the component level presentation web scripts, and the other is client-side JavaScript.

Calling a web script from the presentation web script JavaScript controller

Alfresco Share renders the user interface using the presentation web scripts. These presentation web scripts make a call to the repository web script to render the repository data. Repository web script is called before the component rendering file (for example, `get.html.ftl`) loads.

In out-of-the-box Alfresco installation, you should be able to see the components' presentation web script available under `tomcat\webapps\share\WEB-INF\classes\alfresco\site-webscripts`.

When developing a custom component, you will be required to write a presentation web script. A presentation web script will make a call to the repository web script. You can make a call to the repository web script as follows:

```
var reponse = remote.call("url of web script as defined in description
document");
var obj = eval('(' + response + ')');
```

In the preceding code snippet, we have used the out-of-the-box available `remote` object to make a repository web script call. The important thing to notice is that we have to provide the URL of the web script as defined in the description document. There is no need to provide the initial part such as host or port name, application name, and service path the way we use while calling web script from a web browser. Once the response is received, web script response can be parsed with the use of the `eval` function.

In the out-of-the-box code of Alfresco Share, you can find the presentation web scripts invoking the repository web scripts, as we have seen in the previous code snippet. For example, take a look at the `main()` method in the `site-members.get.js` file, which is available at the `tomcat\webapps\share\components\site-members` location inside your Alfresco installed directory. You can take a look at the other JavaScript controller implementation for out-of-the-box presentation web scripts available at `tomcat\webapps\share\WEB-INF\classes\alfresco\site-webscripts` making repository web script calls using the previously mentioned technique.

 When specifying the path to provide references to the out-of-the-box web scripts, it is mentioned starting with `tomcat\webapps`. This location is available in your Alfresco installation directory.

Invoking a web script from client-side JavaScript

The client-side JavaScript control file can be associated with components in Alfresco Share. If you need to make a repository web script call, you can do this from the client-side JavaScript control files generally located at `tomcat\webapps\share\components`. There are different ways you can make a repository web script call using a YUI-based client-side JavaScript file. The following are some of the ways to invoke web script from client-side JavaScript files. References are also provided along with each of the ways to look in the Alfresco out-of-the-box implementation to understand its usage practically:

- `Alfresco.util.Ajax.request`: Take a look at `tomcat\webapps\share\components\console\groups.js` and refer to the `_removeUser` function.

- `Alfresco.util.Ajax.jsonRequest`: Take a look at `tomcat\webapps\share\components\documentlibrary\documentlist.js` and refer to the `onOptionSelect` function.

- `Alfresco.util.Ajax.jsonGet`: To directly make a call to get web script, take a look at `tomcat\webapps\share\components\console\groups.js` and refer to the `getParentGroups` function.

- `YAHOO.util.Connect.asyncRequest`: Take a look at `tomcat\webapps\share\components\documentlibrary\tree.js` and refer to the `_sortNodeChildren` function.

 In `alfresco.js` located at `tomcat\webapps\share\js`, the wrapper implementation of `YAHOO.util.Connect.asyncRequest` is provided and various available methods such as the ones we saw in the preceding list, `Alfresco.util.Ajax.request`, `Alfresco.util.Ajax.jsonRequest`, and `Alfresco.util.Ajax.jsonGet` can be found in `alfresco.js`. Hence, the first three options in the previous list internally make a call using the `YAHOO.util.Connect.asyncRequest` (the last option in the previous list) only.

Calling a web script from the command line

Sometimes while working on your project, it might be required that from the Linux machine you need to invoke a web script or create a shell script to invoke a web script. It is possible to invoke a web script from the command line using cURL, which is a valuable tool to use while working on web scripts.

You can install cURL on Linux, Mac, or Windows and execute a web script from the command line. Refer to `http://curl.haxx.se/` for more details on cURL. You will be required to install cURL first. On Linux, you can install cURL using `apt-get`. On Mac, you should be able to install cURL through MacPorts and on Windows using Cygwin you can install cURL.

Once cURL is installed, you can invoke web script from the command line as follows:

```
curl -u admin:admin "http://localhost:8080/alfresco/service/
helloworld?name=Ramesh"
```

This will display the web script response.

Calling a web script from JSR-168 portals and the JSF page

The Web script framework in Alfresco provides a helper to make a call to Alfresco web scripts from some of the client environments that do not know HTTP. Hence, it makes it easy to invoke web scripts from such an environment and a web script will be invoked using a mechanism that is familiar to the calling environment. In order to allow JSR-168 portals and JSF pages to naturally invoke a web script as per their environment, the web script framework in Alfresco has provided helpers for them. Let's take a look at them and how they work at a high level.

Calling a web script from JSR-168 portals

It is possible to invoke an Alfresco web script as if it were a JSR-portlet. We will take a look at the configuration required to be done in Alfresco for this. Entry for the web script should be provided in `portlet.xml`. The web script URL should be configured as a JSR-portal URL under the `scripturl` param in order to be able to invoke the web script as a portlet. Basically it has `/alfresco/168s` added before the URL defined in the web script description document.

For example, you can take a look at the out-of-the-box implementation of the `mytasks` web script available at `tomcat\webapps\alfresco\WEB-INF\classes\alfresco\templates\webscripts\org\alfresco\portlets\mytasks.get.desc.xml` and `mytasks.get.html.ftl`. If you are using Alfresco Community 5, these two files are located under the `alfresco` package inside `alfresco-remote-api-*.jar`. Entry for `mytasks web script` as a portlet is configured in `tomcat\webapps\alfresco\WEB-INF\portlet.xml`.

Calling a web script from the JSF page

It is possible to invoke a web script from the JSF page as if it were a tag library. There is a tag implementation provided in Alfresco to have JSF pages invoke web scripts. It's available in `repo.tld` located at the `tomcat\webapps\alfresco\WEB-INF` location in your Alfresco installation.

Take a look at `tomcat\webapps\alfresco\jsp\dashboards\dashlets\mytasks-webscript.jsp` to get an understanding of how it is used.

Dealing with client limitations

One of the limitations would be that not all clients can make all the HTTP calls. It might be possible that it is only restricted to GET or POST calls. The web script framework in Alfresco provides a way to tunnel an HTTP method using a POST method and using it, you can invoke other HTTP method calls. This can be done using the `X-HTTP-Method-Override` header in the HTTP request with the value as the method name, for example, GET. An alternative way is to specify `alf_method` as a query string parameter.

Another client limitation could be that not all clients can gracefully handle HTTP codes for non-success. In such cases, there is a mechanism to force the HTTP response to specify success in the response header. The response body still represents the content as if a non-success status has been received, which allows the client to know about the error code or message provided by the web script, if any. In order to be able to gracefully handle the HTTP code for non-success scenarios, it is possible to forcefully specify the success in the HTTP response each time by setting the `alf-force-success-response` header with a value of `true` on the HTTP request.

Summary

In this chapter, we have gained an understanding about the different ways to invoke a web script, for example, from the web browser. Using the add-ons available for the web browser, web scripts can be invoked. We have seen different ways to invoke web scripts from a standalone Java class. We have also gone through how to invoke web scripts from Spring-based services and from the command line. We gained knowledge about the possibility of invoking web scripts as JSR-168 portlets and JSF pages. We also saw how the web script framework in Alfresco provides us with ways to deal with some of the limitations of the calling clients.

We are going to learn how to develop Java-backed web scripts in the next chapter.

6
Creating Java-backed Web Scripts

In this chapter, we will cover how to create Java-backed Alfresco web scripts in detail. In order to do this, we will cover the following:

- Defining a sample use case scenario first
- Getting ready and identifying the required components to be developed
- Developing a Java-backed web script step by step
- Deploying and registering the web script
- Testing the web script as per the use case scenario
- Understanding the difference between the web script framework's helper classes to create a Java-backed controller
- Looking at some useful pointers to use controllers effectively

When developing web scripts in Alfresco, there are two choices to write the controller implementation for a web script: a JavaScript-backed controller and Java-backed controller. Depending on your preference, you can choose to develop controller implementation from these two when required. With a JavaScript-backed controller, the development cycle can get faster compared to a Java-backed controller. There is a wide range of things that you can do with the Alfresco JavaScript API inside the JavaScript-based controller. However, there might be times when this is not enough for what you want to implement for your business requirement. In such cases, you can use the Java-backed web script, wherein it is possible to use all the Alfresco services such as NodeService, SearchService, ContentService, and others, and the web script can be built up as required.

While working on projects where you might end up developing a large number of web scripts, you have to decide which type of controller implementation you will be implementing based upon the feasibility of the project execution. You can choose to develop JavaScript controller-based web scripts to speed up the development and develop Java-backed web scripts only in the scenario when a JavaScript API does not fit your requirement. Alternatively, you can always use Java-backed web scripts in order to have a standardized development approach for your project.

It is important to have an understanding of implementing web scripts with both types of controllers. We have already seen how a JavaScript-backed controller can be used for a web script when we created a hello world web script earlier. Now, it's time for a Java-backed web script. In this chapter, we will implement a Java-backed web script in Alfresco for a sample use case so that you will get an understanding about how to create a web script in Alfresco step by step that has a Java-backed controller implementation. You can then develop Java-backed web scripts for the business requirements in your project as required.

Use case scenario

We will take a very simple scenario to get an overall understanding of creating a web script with a Java-backed controller. Our main objective is to understand how to create Java-backed web scripts and how to use Alfresco APIs inside the Java-backed controller. Let's get started.

You must be aware that Alfresco stores the metadata of the content in a database and stores the actual content on a filesystem. Now, once the content is available in Alfresco, you might be interested to know its location and find out where it actually resides on the filesystem. So, the next time you are discussing content in Alfresco with someone, you can actually showcase the mapping of content in Alfresco with its actual physical location on filesystem under content store.

Also, while working on projects with external application integration with Alfresco, you might at some point in time want to know the size of the content as well, along with its location on the filesystem.

Let's take this as our use case scenario to build our Java-backed web script. We basically want to create a web script in Alfresco that will provide the actual location on the filesystem for the given node and size of its content.

Web script functionality at a high level

After understanding the overall scenario that we want to achieve, let's understand how this web script will work at a high level:

- A parameter `nodeid` needs to be passed as a request argument to the web script.

- The web script will be accessed by authenticated users only.

- If a user has at the minimum read access to a given node, then only the physical location of the filesystem and content size will be provided for the node.

- A response will be provided in JSON as well as XML format. The format can be specified at the time of invoking the web script.

Getting ready

Let's just brush up on our knowledge of web script building blocks and identify the components that need to be created for this web script as follows:

- Each web script needs to have a description document. So, the first step is to create a web script description document.

- The web script needs to return a response in the XML and JSON formats, so it is necessary to provide the response template to render an XML response and a response template to render a JSON response.

- The entire logic to get the filesystem location and size will reside in the web script controller. In this case, a Java-backed web script controller needs to be created for business logic processing.

- In order to register a Java-backed controller with the web script, a spring configuration is required. Hence, a spring context file needs to be created to register a Java-backed controller with the web script. It is not necessary to create a new spring context file always. You can have a context file based on the logical module of your system and all the web scripts belonging to this module could be registered in that context file.

For this web script, you can use your favorite editor to create the required files for the web script and develop the controller Java class. We will cover setting up the development environment using Maven in *Chapter 9, Mavenizing Web Scripts*. In this chapter, we will mainly aim to get an understanding of how to implement a Java-backed web script. You need to have `spring-webscripts-*.jar` and `alfresco-data-model-*.jar` added in your class path in order to be able to compile the controller Java class. Both these JARs can be found at the `tomcat\webapps\alfresco\WEB-INF\lib` location in your Alfresco installation. The * symbol in the JAR name refers to the version number.

Creating a description document

As the primary purpose of the web script is to return the content location, let's use the web script ID as `contentlocation`. We will use the HTTP GET method as we are going to retrieve the information for a node.

As a first step, create a description document for the web script. Create a file named `contentlocation.get.desc.xml` that has the following content:

```
<webscript>
  <shortname>Get content location and size</shortname>
  <description>Gets the physical location for the content and size
    of the content</description>
  <url>/getContentLocation?nodeid={nodeid}</url>
  <url>/getContentLocation.json?nodeid={nodeid}</url>
  <url>/getContentLocation.xml?nodeid={nodeid}</url>
  <format default="json">extension</format>
  <authentication>user</authentication>
</webscript>
```

Let's understand what we have just done. We have created a description document that provides a human-readable name and brief information about the web script in the `shortname` and `description` tags respectively.

We have defined three URLs that can be used to invoke a web script. The first one is the default URL and the other two are explicitly mentioned to get a response in JSON and XML formats respectively. Please note that the first and second URL will produce the same output.

The default response format is specified as `json`. The value `extension` for the `format` tag mentions that a response content type can be specified as an extension to the web script ID while invoking the web script.

Also most importantly, a web script expects an argument named `nodeid` when the web script is invoked.

Creating a response template

As a rule of thumb for a web script, we have to follow the naming convention as expected by the web script framework in Alfresco. As the web script is supposed to return the response in the JSON and XML formats, we need to create two response templates for the web script. Following the naming conventions, there are two files to be created — `contentlocation.get.json.ftl` and `contentlocation.get.xml.ftl` as response templates. Return `filesystem_location` and `size` in the response as follows:

1. To create a JSON response template, create a file named `contentlocation.get.json.ftl` that has the following content:

```
{
  "content" :
  {
    "filesystem_location" : "${contentFSLocation}",
    "size" : ${contentSize}
  }
}
```

2. To create an XML response template, create a file named `contentlocation.get.xml.ftl` that has the following content:

```
<?xml version="1.0" encoding="UTF-8"?>
<content>
  <filesystem_location>${contentFSLocation}
  </filesystem_location>
  <size>${contentSize}</size>
</content>
```

We have just created two response templates as required to return the output for the web script. The names used inside `${}` in the preceding code snippets are the model variable names to be set from the controller class. Make sure that while implementing a controller, the model variable names are set with the same name as used in the response templates.

Creating a Java controller

Now it's time to do some Java coding. Before we start the actual coding, it's always a good idea to quickly identify the logic that has to be taken care of by the code we are going to write. This exercise really does help a lot.

Controller logic at a high level

In order to develop a controller for this scenario, let's take a look at the implementation logic that we will include in the Java-backed controller at a high level:

- A controller will expect `nodeid` as an input parameter
- Check whether the given node is present in the repository
- Check whether the user has at least read permissions on the given node
- Get the filesystem location for the given node
- Get the size on the filesystem for the given node
- Prepare the model object and return it to the FTL response template

Let's code it!

Let's perform the following steps to create a Java-backed controller implementation for the web script that will perform all the required logic as mentioned in the previous section:

1. Create a new class, `com.example.content.ContentLocationWebScript`. It's generally a good idea to provide a descriptive naming style and classify the web scripts under appropriate packages. This will be useful in a scenario where a large number of web scripts are to be developed. As this is going to be a content-related web script, we have kept it under the `com.example.content` package and named it `ContentLocationWebScript`.

2. The Java class `ContentLocationWebScript` you have just created must extend `org.springframework.extensions.webscripts.DeclarativeWebScript` as follows:

   ```
   public class ContentLocationWebScript extends org.springframework.
   extensions.webscripts.DeclarativeWebScript {
   ```

3. We are going to use the Node service, which is basically used to perform node-related operations such as create, update, delete, set properties, and get properties in Alfresco, to get the details about the filesystem location. We will use the Permission service to identify whether a user has read access. Now the next step is to provide the declaration for them. Both of them will be injected as a Spring dependency as follows:

   ```
   private NodeService nodeService;
   private PermissionService permissionService;
   ```

4. Next, let's write the actual logic for the controller. The whole logic will go inside the `executeImpl` method. The first thing to do inside this method is get the `nodeid` request parameter value as follows:

```
@Override
protected Map<String, Object> executeImpl(WebScriptRequest req,
Status status, Cache cache) {
    String nodeId = req.getParameter("nodeid");
```

5. As `nodeid` is a mandatory parameter for this web script, make sure that you have received the value for `nodeid`. At the controller end, this needs to be taken care of and proceed only if the value for the `nodeid` parameter has been provided. If the `nodeid` is not provided, then the controller will set the error response code. If it is provided, then prepare `NodeRef` based on the `nodeid`:

```
if (null == nodeId || "".equals(nodeId)) {
    status.setCode(Status.STATUS_BAD_REQUEST);
    status.setRedirect(true);
    return null;
}
NodeRef contentNodeRef = new NodeRef("workspace://SpacesStore/" +
nodeId);
```

 In a scenario when `status.setRedirect` is set as `true`, if a custom status response template is provided for the status code, then it will be rendered; otherwise, the default status response template provided by the web script framework in Alfresco will be rendered displaying the information about status. If `status.setRedirect` is set as `false`, then the status code will be set on response; however, the response template for the requested format will be rendered.

6. The next thing is to check whether `NodeRef` is present in the repository. If `NodeRef` does not exist, then the controller will set the relevant error response code. A controller will only proceed if `NodeRef` is available in the repository as follows:

```
if (!nodeService.exists(contentNodeRef)) {
    status.setCode(Status.STATUS_NOT_FOUND);
    status.setRedirect(true);
    return null;
}
```

7. Now, check whether the user has at least read access on the given `noderef`. A controller will only proceed further if a user has at least read permissions on the node, otherwise the controller will set the appropriate error response code.

```
if (permissionService.hasPermission(contentNodeRef,
PermissionService.READ) != AccessStatus.ALLOWED){
  status.setCode(Status.STATUS_FORBIDDEN);
  status.setRedirect(true);
  return null;
}
```

8. The next step is to get the filesystem location and size for the content as follows:

```
ContentData contentData = (ContentData) nodeService.
getProperty(contentNodeRef, ContentModel.PROP_CONTENT);
String contentFileLocation = contentData.getContentUrl();
Long contentSize = contentData.getSize();
```

9. Create and set the model object to render the information in response as follows:

```
Map<String, Object> model = new HashMap<String, Object>();
model.put("contentFSLocation", contentFileLocation);
model.put("contentSize", contentSize);
return model;
}
```

10. At the end of the class, provide the setter methods for the node service and permission service as follows:

```
public void setNodeService(NodeService nodeService) {
  this.nodeService = nodeService;
}

public void setPermissionService(PermissionService
permissionService) {
    this.permissionService = permissionService;
  }
}
```

11. Save the class, and the Java controller implementation is now ready.

We have just created a Java-backed controller implementation that will perform the specified logic processing prior to returning the content location on the filesystem and size of content. We also used the node service and permission service in the controller.

Configuring the controller for the web script

Once the Java controller is ready, it needs to be configured for the web script so that the web script framework in Alfresco can get to know that this Java class is the controller for the `contentlocation` web script. This can be done by creating a spring context file and adding the entry for the Java class in it.

Create a file `custom-example-webscripts-context.xml` that has the following content:

```xml
<?xml version="1.0" encoding="UTF-8"?>
<!DOCTYPE beans PUBLIC '-//SPRING//DTD BEAN//EN' 'http://www.
springframework.org/dtd/spring-beans.dtd'>
<beans>
  <bean id="webscript.example.contentlocation.get"
    class="com.example.content.ContentLocationWebScript"
    parent="webscript">
      <property name="nodeService" ref="nodeService" />
      <property name="permissionService"
        ref="permissionService" />
  </bean>
</beans>
```

We created a spring context file to associate the Java controller with the `contentlocation` web script in order to let the web script framework in Alfresco know that the `ContentLocationWebscript` Java class is the controller for the `contentlocation` web script. This is done by following the appropriate naming convention while providing a bean entry in the context file.

The most important thing is to specify the correct bean ID. The naming convention that needs to be followed is `webscript.package.webscriptid.httpmethod`.

Hence, the way it needs to be built is, that if the web script description file resides at `templates\webscripts\example\contentlocation.get.desc.xml` location, then the bean ID would be `webscript.example.contentlocation.get`. Following this naming convention is a must in order to register the class as a controller for the web script. If you fail to do so, the web script framework in Alfresco will not be able to register the class as a web script controller and when you try to execute the web script, the controller code will not get called.

In the bean entry in context file, the class name would be the fully qualified class name for the Java controller. For example, in the preceding bean entry for our Java controller, we provided the class as `com.example.content.ContentLocationWebScript` that is basically the fully qualified class name for our Java controller. The parent attribute would be `webscript`. You must take extra care when specifying the parent attribute, it must be set to `webscript` and not `webscripts`.

Deploying the web script

The web script components are now ready. In order to make them work together, these need to be deployed now. In your Alfresco installed directory, perform the following steps:

1. Create a folder named `example` at the location `tomcat\shared\classes\alfresco\extension\templates\webscripts`.

2. Put `contentlocation.get.desc.xml`, `contentlocation.get.json.ftl`, and `contentlocation.get.xml.ftl` at the location `tomcat\shared\classes\alfresco\extension\templates\webscripts\example`.

3. Put `custom-example-webscripts-context.xml` at the location `tomcat\shared\classes\alfresco\extension`.

4. Create folders `com | example | content` at the location `tomcat\webapps\alfresco\WEB-INF\classes`.

5. Put the compiled Java class `ContentLocationWebscript.class` at the location `tomcat\webapps\alfresco\WEB-INF\classes\com\example\content`.

6. Restart the server.

Registering the web script

As we just restarted the server, on a server startup, the web script gets registered. Now in order to confirm this, go to the URL `http://localhost:8080/alfresco/service/index`, provide a username and password on authentication pop up, and click on the **Browse by Web Script Package** button. Search for `example` and click on it. The newly registered web script's index will be displayed as follows:

```
Get content location and size
GET /alfresco/service/getContentLocation?nodeid={nodeid}
GET /alfresco/service/getContentLocation.json?nodeid={nodeid}
GET /alfresco/service/getContentLocation.xml?nodeid={nodeid}
Description: Gets the physical location for the content and size of
the content
Authentication: user
```

```
Transaction: required
Format Style: extension
Default Format: json
Id: example/contentlocation.get
Description:classpath:alfresco/extension/templates/webscripts/example/
contentlocation.get.desc.xml
```

Testing the web script

It's now time to test the functionality of the web script we have just created. We basically want to make sure that the logic we have incorporated in the Java-backed controller is working as expected.

In order to test the web script, upload some content (say an image) in the Alfresco repository first. Make a note of its `nodeid`. In order to get the `nodeid` of uploaded content after the content is uploaded using Alfresco Share, just take the mouse pointer to the content name and then right-click on it and click on **Copy link location**. Paste this link somewhere in a text editor and copy the value after `workspace://SpacesStore`; this forms the `nodeid`. Now, create two users and give one of them consumer access and do not give any permission to the other user on this content. Make sure inherit permission is also unchecked.

Now, with any of the two users, start testing the web script.

Test case 1 – mandatory check

The `nodeid` is a mandatory argument for the web script we created. As a first test case, let's test invoking a web script without passing the `nodeid` as a request parameter. Hence, the first test would be not to pass the `nodeid` parameter in the web script request. Hit the `http://localhost:8080/alfresco/service/getContentLocation` URL in the browser.

As we specified the default format as JSON, the JSON response will be rendered as shown in the following code snippet. Since we have not created a custom status template and used `status.setRedirect` as `true`, the default status response template provided by the web script framework in Alfresco is rendered. The same output will also be displayed if the JSON format had been requested explicitly while invoking the web script request as `http://localhost:8080/alfresco/service/getContentLocation.json`.

The following is the web script output:

```
{
  "status" :
  {
    "code" : 400,
    "name" : "Bad Request",
    "description" : "Request sent by the client was syntactically
      incorrect."
  }
}
```

If you want to take a look at the XML response, then go to the following URL
`http://localhost:8080/alfresco/service/getContentLocation.xml`
and the following would be the response:

```
<response>
  <status>
    <code>400</code>
    <name>Bad Request</name>
  </status>
</response>
```

Test case 2 – invalid argument value

As the second test case, we will test the web script by providing an invalid value for the `nodeid` parameter. While invoking the web script, provide the `nodeid`; however, give an invalid value for the `nodeid` and check the response for both the JSON and XML format.

For the JSON response, go to `http://localhost:8080/alfresco/service/getContentLocation.json?nodeid=invalidnode` or `http://localhost:8080/alfresco/service/getContentLocation?nodeid=invalidnode`.

The output in the JSON format would appear as follows:

```
{
  "status" :
  {
    "code" : 404,
    "name" : "Not Found",
    "description" : "Requested resource is not available."
  }
}
```

For an XML response, go to `http://localhost:8080/alfresco/service/` `getContentLocation.xml?nodeid=invalidnode`. It will display the response in the XML format mentioning the 404 status code.

Test case 3 – invalid access

We did a mandatory check for the `nodeid` parameter and tested the web script using an invalid value in the previous test cases. Now, provide the correct value for the `nodeid`, invoke the web script, and provide authentication for the user that does not have access to the content. Our third test case is to test the web script with the user for whom we have not provided any access to the content. Check for the JSON and XML response as we did in previous test cases. It should give 403 as the status code showing forbidden access.

Test case 4 – test with valid data

Now it's time to test the web script with some valid test data, which means a user that has access to the content and a valid `nodeid` should be passed in the web script request parameter. Check the response for both the JSON and XML format by going to the web script URL, providing a valid `nodeid` as the argument. You should now be able to see the response that shows the physical location of the content on the filesystem and its size. The following displays the sample XML response:

```
<content>
  <filesystem_location>store://2014/7/20/xx/x/xxxxxx.bin
    </filesystem_location>
  <size>500</size>
</content>
```

Once you get the response, you can try to navigate to the path received in the `filesystem_location` tag. The directory structure can be found under the `alf_data` location mentioned in `alfresco-global.properties`, which can be located at `tomcat\shared\classes` inside your Alfresco installed directory. The content size is displayed in bytes. It is important to understand that we do not update or delete anything in `alf_data` and its subfolders as it might corrupt the repository.

So, for any content in Alfresco, you can find its size and its physical location on the filesystem.

DeclarativeWebScript versus AbstractWebScript

The web script framework in Alfresco provides two different helper classes from which the Java-backed controller can be derived. It's important to understand the difference between them.

The first helper class is the one we used while developing the web script in this chapter, `org.springframework.extensions.webscripts.DeclarativeWebScript`. The second one is `org.springframework.extensions.webscripts.AbstractWebScript`.

`DeclarativeWebScript` in turn only extends the `AbstractWebScript` class.

If the Java-backed controller is derived from `DeclarativeWebScript`, then execution assistance is provided by the `DeclarativeWebScript` class. This helper class basically encapsulates the execution of the web script and checks if any controller written in JavaScript is associated with the web script or not. If any JavaScript controller is found for the web script, then this helper class will execute it. This class will locate the associated response template of the web script for the requested format and will pass the populated model object to the response template.

For the controller extending `DeclarativeWebScript`, the controller logic for a web script should be provided in the `Map<String, Object> executeImpl(WebScriptRequest req, Status status, Cache cache)` method. Most of the time while developing a Java-backed web script, the controller will extend `DeclarativeWebScript` only.

`AbstractWebScript` does not provide execution assistance in the way `DeclarativeWebScript` does. It gives full control over the entire execution process to the derived class and allows the extending class to decide how the output is to be rendered. One good example of this is the `DeclarativeWebScript` class itself. It extends the `AbstractWebScript` class and provides a mechanism to render the response using FTL templates. In a scenario like streaming the content, there won't be any need for a response template; instead, the content itself needs to be rendered directly. In this case, the Java-backed controller class can extend from `AbstractWebScript`.

If a web script has both a JavaScript-based controller and a Java-backed controller, then:

- If a Java-backed controller is derived from DeclarativeWebScript, then first the Java-backed controller will get executed and then the control would be passed to the JavaScript-backed controller prior to returning the model object to the response template.

- If the Java-backed controller is derived from AbstractWebScript, then, only the Java-backed controller will be executed. The JavaScript controller will not get executed.

Using controllers smartly

It's always suggested to use either a Java-backed controller or JavaScript-backed controller for a web script and both controllers should not be used together. However, let's take a look at some scenarios where you can leverage using both the controllers for a web script and solve some critical issues.

Consider a scenario where in a production system, you already have a web script that has a Java-backed controller extending DeclarativeWebScript and returns some output. Now, as a part of fixing a critical issue, there is a need to return additional information in the web script response and you did not have the option to restart the production server as server downtime could impact the customer business. In this scenario, you can write an additional JavaScript controller for your web script, set the additional information in the model object, and modify the response template to include the newly added information. Register the web script and web script should now return additional information as well along with the earlier output. Hence, we can say we have done a kind of chaining of the controller execution. Think of this as being similar to servlet chaining. This is the power of the web script framework in Alfresco that makes it easy to solve critical issues very effectively.

Another scenario could be that you want to have a filter kind of functionality. Before executing the JavaScript-backed web script, you need to perform some business logic communication with the external application, and based on its output, you need to process the remaining part of the web script. Here, you can think of developing the Java controller extending DeclarativeWebScript. It's easier to have spring services wired for a Java controller. Using this, make a call to the external application and set a model object. Now, in the JavaScript-based controller, based on the value of the model object available from Java controller, continue the processing. In this way, a servlet filter kind of functionality can be achieved for web scripts.

Summary

In this chapter, we understood in detail how to develop a Java-backed web script in Alfresco. We took a sample use case scenario and first identified the requisites and identified the logic implementation to be included in the controller before actually implementing the web script. We implemented the web script description document, response templates for JSON and XML, Java-backed controller, and associated the controller with the web script step by step. We then deployed the web script and registered the web script to the web script framework.

Later, we tested the web script in order to see its output in different test scenarios to test the logic implemented in the controller. Finally, we understood the differences between the two helper classes provided by the web script framework in Alfresco to implement the Java-backed controller for a web script. Also, we had a look at some quick helpful pointers to understand in which scenarios we can have both Java and JavaScript types of controllers. Now, you have gained the required knowledge to implement any complex Java-backed web script to meet your business requirements.

In the next chapter, we will take a look at JavaScript-based web scripts in detail.

7
Understanding JavaScript-based Web Scripts in Detail

In this chapter, we will cover the following topics:

- What can you do with JavaScript APIs?
- How do you find available JavaScript APIs in Alfresco?
- Available root objects to access JavaScript APIs
- Other root objects provided by the web script framework in Alfresco
- A few code examples of some common functionalities in a JavaScript controller
- Creating your own root object

The web script framework in Alfresco makes it easy to create, access, update, and delete content residing in the repository using JavaScript-backed web scripts. The JavaScript-backed web script will be very helpful when you need to do some kind of hotfixes without bringing down the production system. Another cool feature of JavaScript-backed web scripts is that you can have them deployed in the repository and can directly edit them in line using the Alfresco user interface. There is no need to depend on any specific editor while developing web scripts that have a JavaScript-backed controller. You can use any of your favorite editors to create them. The major advantage of using a JavaScript-backed web script is that it speeds up the development cycle of web scripts. You need not worry about compiling them the way you do with your Java-backed web scripts. While developing JavaScript-backed web scripts, you can leverage the Alfresco provided JavaScript APIs. There is a wide range of APIs provided by Alfresco to make repository access easy and convenient from JavaScript-controller-backed web scripts.

In this chapter, first we will find out the possible things that you can do using JavaScript APIs. We will learn how to identify the available JavaScript APIs in Alfresco. We are going to take a look at the root objects available in Alfresco. This will help us access the available JavaScript API and effectively develop web scripts in less time; also, it will make it easier to interact with the Alfresco repository. We will also look at other helpful root objects provided by the web script framework in Alfresco. We will see few code examples that will help you understand how you can make use of Alfresco JavaScript APIs in your web script. At the end, we will go through the steps to understand how to create a custom JavaScript extension, which is a very important and useful thing to know.

Understanding what you can do with the JavaScript API

While developing web scripts in Alfresco, the repository JavaScript APIs provided by Alfresco will help you perform a lot of the following actions at a high level as listed in the following list:

- Creating a folder
- Creating content
- Making a copy of a node
- Moving a node from one location to another
- Deleting a node
- Finding a node
- Performing searches against a repository

- Traversing through the node hierarchy
- Modifying properties on a node
- Adding or removing an aspect on a node
- Creating, modifying, or removing associations for a node
- Getting permission for a node
- Modifying permission for a node
- Creating and removing groups
- Creating and removing users

Basically, you can think of Alfresco JavaScript APIs as a wrapper to access Alfresco services from the JavaScript-backed controller. Alfresco uses the Mozilla Rhino JavaScript engine for Java, which allows JavaScript files to access Alfresco Java objects using a simple bean-style approach in scripting. Also, this makes it simpler to develop JavaScript (ECMA Script) 1.6 compatible files to create, update, retrieve, and delete Alfresco repository objects using Alfresco JavaScript APIs.

JavaScript APIs in Alfresco

As a developer, you must always be interested in debugging through the code in order to get an understanding of its workings instead of directly having the list of APIs and simply using it. So, here we are going to take a look at how to identify JavaScript APIs in Alfresco. Now, let's find the available JavaScript APIs provided by Alfresco that we can use in a JavaScript controller while developing web scripts.

Identifying JavaScript APIs

In the Alfresco code base, the simplest way to identify any JavaScript API is through the bean definition, where it will have the parent specified as `baseJavaScriptExtension`. The way the bean entry works is – any JavaScript API can be accessed through the root object defined for it. The property name defined under the `extensionName` property is the root object to access the relevant API.

Let's discuss the bean definition entry for a JavaScript API in order to get a better understanding of how the JavaScript API is defined. The following is the code snippet of one such API available in Alfresco, which will give you a clear understanding of how a JavaScript API is available and how you can use it in the controller:

```
<bean id="actionsScript" parent="baseJavaScriptExtension" class="org.
alfresco.repo.jscript.Actions">
  <property name="extensionName">
    <value>actions</value>
```

```
    </property>
    <property name="serviceRegistry">
      <ref bean="ServiceRegistry"/>
    </property>
  </bean>
```

The following are some important points we can understand from this code snippet:

- This has the parent defined as `baseJavaScriptExtension`.

- All the methods that are available to the JavaScript controller are defined in the Java class `org.alfresco.repo.jscript.Actions`.

- Dependency of any Alfresco services can be injected to the bean definition, which can be used in the Java class to perform an operation against the repository.

- The JavaScript controller will use the value provided under the `extensionName` property in the bean definition to access the methods exposed by the Java class. This value provided under the `extensionName` property is referred to as a root object available in the JavaScript controller to access the JavaScript API.

Now, with this understanding, you have the key to using JavaScript APIs for your web script. You just unlocked how Java objects are being accessed from the JavaScript controller.

Root objects to access JavaScript APIs

Now you understand how to identify JavaScript APIs in the Alfresco code base, let's take a look at all the root objects available to access JavaScript APIs from the JavaScript controller. In your Alfresco installed directory, you can find the generally used JavaScript APIs defined in `script-services-context.xml` at `tomcat\webapps\alfresco\WEB-INF\classes\alfresco`.

If you are using Alfresco Community 5, `script-services-context.xml` can be located inside `alfresco-repository-*.jar` under the `alfresco` package. In the following table, the entries are mentioned first with the name of the root object followed by the fully qualified name of the class, which has the implementation of the API methods and a brief description of the root object:

Root object	Name of the class	Description
logger	`org.alfresco.repo.jscript.ScriptLogger`	This can be used to log the required details that can be used while debugging an issue
utils	`org.alfresco.repo.jscript.ScriptUtils`	This provides some generic useful utility methods
test	`org.alfresco.repo.jscript.ScriptTestUtils`	This utility class provides some test methods
actions	`org.alfresco.repo.jscript.Actions`	This provides a way to execute actions on a node
imap	`org.alfresco.repo.jscript.Imap`	This provides access to imap methods such as get the imap home for user
search	`org.alfresco.repo.jscript.Search`	This provides way to search data against the Alfresco repository
classification	`org.alfresco.repo.jscript.Classification`	This provides the methods to create and access categories
people	`org.alfresco.repo.jscript.People`	This provides access to the person and group, and provides a way to manipulate them
session	`org.alfresco.repo.jscript.Session`	This provides the current user's authentication ticket
avm	`org.alfresco.repo.jscript.AVM`	This provides helper methods to access AVM objects
crossRepoCopy	`org.alfresco.repo.jscript.CrossRepositoryCopy`	This provides support for cross-repository copy
workflow	`org.alfresco.repo.workflow.jscript.WorkflowManager`	This allows you to create workflows and interact with workflows in Alfresco
presence	`org.alfresco.repo.jscript.Presence`	This provides a way to query the current online status of a person

Root object	Name of the class	Description
activities	`org.alfresco.repo.activities.script.Activity`	This provides methods to post activity and feed control
appUtils	`org.alfresco.repo.jscript.ApplicationScriptUtils`	This provides some methods that could be useful for an external application

Apart from this, if you search the XML files in the Alfresco installed directory for `parent="baseJavaScriptExtension"`, you will get an additional list of root objects and its relevant classes in other context files. Here are the other available root objects defined as mentioned earlier: `actionTrackingService`, `groups`, `formService`, `invitations`, `preferenceService`, `ratingService`, `renditionService`, `replicationService`, `siteService`, `slingshotDocLib`, `taggingService`, `thumbnailService`, `transfer`, `webprojects`, `cmisserver`, `commentService`, `bulkFSImport`, `jmx`, and `admIndexCheckService`.

To learn more, you should do a brief exercise and find the related Java classes for these root objects and go through them. This exercise will make you familiar with the available methods that you can use in the JavaScript-backed controller.

While developing a JavaScript-backed controller, the basic concept is simple; take a look at the methods available in the defined Java class for the JavaScript API and access those methods with the name given under the `extensionName` property.

Other available root objects

We have seen the root objects that have the API methods implemented in the Java classes. There are some other default root objects provided by the web script framework in Alfresco that you can use in the JavaScript controller of a web script. We saw the different classes that get involved in executing web scripts while looking at a behind-the-scenes implementation of web script execution in *Chapter 3, Understanding the Web Script Framework*. You might want to go through the web script framework classes in `spring-webscripts-*.jar` and `alfresco-remote-api-*.jar` to find out in detail how these root objects are being made available in the JavaScript controller. The following are the available root objects from different classes of a web script framework:

The root objects from `AbstractWebScript` are shown in the following table:

Root object	Name of the class/object	Description
webscript	`org.springframework. extensions.webscripts. Description`	This provides information about the currently executing web script
format	`org.springframework. extensions.webscripts. FormatModel`	This represents the selected format of the rendered response
args	This is a map object	This holds the arguments that are passed to the web script
argM	This is a map object	This holds the multivalued parameter arguments passed to the web script
headers	This is a map object	This holds the request header values passed to the web script
headersM	This is a map object	This holds the multivalued request header values passed to the web script
guest	This is a Boolean value	This indicates whether the current user is a guest user or not
url	`org.springframework. extensions.webscripts. URLModel`	This provides access to the web script URL and its parts
msg	`org.springframework. extensions.webscripts. ScriptMessage`	This provides access to localized messages for a web script
config	`org.springframework. extensions.webscripts. ScriptConfigModel`	This provides access to the configuration document for a web script
formdata	object	This holds the data submitted in a form for a web script
requestbody	`Content`	This represents the content of the request body
json	Object, `JSONArray`, or `JSONObject`	This is generated from the posted JSON request to the web script

The root objects from `DeclarativeWebScript` are shown in the following table:

Root object	Name of the class/object	Description
model	This is a map object	This will be used by the controller to pass the data to the response template
status	`org.springframework.extensions.webscripts.Status`	This represents the response status
cache	`org.springframework.extensions.webscripts.Cache`	This allows the control to cache the response of the web script

The root objects from `TenantRepositoryContainer` are shown in the following table:

Root object	Name of the class/object	Description
cmis	`org.alfresco.repo.cmis.client.CMISLocalConnectionManagerImpl`	This represents CMIS client
paging	`org.alfresco.repo.web.util.paging.Paging`	This is a paging API

The root objects from `RepositoryContainer` are as follows:

Root object	Name of the class/object	Description
roothome	`org.alfresco.repo.jscript.ScriptNode`	This represents the repository root node. Accessible to authenticated users only.
companyhome	`org.alfresco.repo.jscript.ScriptNode`	This represents the company home object. Accessible to authenticated users only.
person	`org.alfresco.repo.jscript.ScriptNode`	This represents the currently authenticated user.
userhome	`org.alfresco.repo.jscript.ScriptNode`	This represents the current user's home space.

The root objects from `AbstractRuntimeContainer` are as follows:

Root object	Name of the class/object	Description
server	`org.alfresco.repo.web.scripts.` `RepositoryServerModel`	This provides server details
atom	`org.springframework.extensions.` `webscripts.atom.AtomService`	This is used to parse and generate atom documents
jsonUtils	`org.springframework.extensions.` `webscripts.json.JSONUtils`	This is used to parse and generate a JSON object
stringUtils	`org.springframework.extensions.` `webscripts.ScriptableUtils`	This is utilities for string

Most of the root objects provided by the web script framework in Alfresco are also available in response templates. If you take a look at web script framework classes, they have the implementation available to provide script root objects and template root objects. Once you have an understanding of how to use root objects in the JavaScript controller, you can also use them in the response template. While developing web scripts, it's always a good approach to perform business logic processing in the controller and populate the model object to display the output on the templates. However, in some scenarios, you might also have to leverage the root objects available for templates when required to form the response.

A must-know ScriptNode API

If you are working on creating web scripts and accessing or manipulating nodes in Alfresco through a JavaScript controller, then you must have an understanding of the `ScriptNode` API. This provides access to various properties of a node and also provides different useful methods for a node in terms of security, thumbnailing, ownership, versioning, tagging, transformation, and so on. You can go through the code for `ScriptNode` to get understanding of the different methods. Its code is available in `alfresco-repository-*.jar` and its fully qualified class name is `org.alfresco.repo.jscript.ScriptNode`.

Similarly, to access the properties of a node and perform various other things in response templates, you should check `org.alfresco.repo.template.TemplateNode` available in `alfresco-repository-*jar`.

Code examples

Now that you have information on the different root objects you can use in the JavaScript controller, let's take a look at some code examples to get a better understanding of how you can put the root objects in action to achieve the required functionality. We will go through some code examples for some of the generic functionalities that every developer will use at some point in time. We will use some of the root objects we have gone through previously.

Creating a folder

Consider a scenario where you have a custom frontend application and Alfresco as the backend repository. Now, you want to have the functionality for the users to create a folder in Alfresco under the company home from the custom frontend. Once the folder is created, you might also want to create some content inside the folder or run some action on the folder. First, our goal is to create a folder under the company home.

To address this, we will create a new web script `foldercreation`, which will accept the argument `foldername` and creates a named folder under the company home and returns the `noderef` value as a response in the XML format. You could use the returned `noderef` further to invoke other web scripts as required, for example, to run an action or create content.

In subsequent sections, you will find the core code snippet that needs to be implemented inside the JavaScript controller and response template in order to achieve the mentioned scenario. You can also go through the code files provided for this chapter in order to see the web script implementation for this web script.

Retrieving explicit arguments

In order to implement this scenario, as the first thing in the JavaScript controller, we need to read the argument `foldername`. Explicit arguments can be retrieved using the `args` root object. So, we will read the argument `foldername` as follows:

```
if (args.foldername != null && args.foldername != "")
```

 If you have implicit arguments provided in the web script URL, then these arguments will not be available using the `args` root object. For them, you can get their values using the `url` root object like in `url.templateArgs.foldername`.

Folder creation under company home

Now, create a folder under the company home. As we saw earlier that companyhome is available as a root object, we can directly use it. It's of the type ScriptNode. So, we can invoke the methods available in the ScriptNode API to create the folder. The CreateFolder() method returns a ScriptNode object; set this object in the model and use it in the response template to get the noderef value from it using the TemplateNode API.

Inside the JavaScript controller, you will have the following lines:

```
var folderName = args.foldername;
model.foldernode = companyhome.createFolder(folderName);
```

In the response template, you will be using the following code:

```
${foldernode.nodeRef}
```

Let's discuss what we have just done. We used the args and companyhome root objects inside the JavaScript controller to read explicit arguments and create a folder respectively. All the available methods from the ScriptNode class can be used with the companyhome object.

Now, we will take a look at some other functionalities as well in order to understand the usage of root objects and JavaScript APIs. We will also take a look at the relevant JavaScript code to achieve the mentioned functionality.

Finding a node

In the preceding example, the web script returned nodeid in the response. It was the nodeid of the folder that was created in the web script. Now, you are interested in using the nodeid returned by the first web script as an input to some other web script. In another web script, you need to pass nodeid as the argument, and on that node, you need to perform some functionalities such as determining whether a user has permission on the node or not, getting the path to the node, getting some property of a node, modifying some property on a node, checking whether some aspect is applied on a node or not, creating content in it, invoking an action, and so on. Before proceeding with any such operations, as the first thing, we need to find out the actual node from the repository based on the nodeid provided. This can be done using the findNode() method accessed by the search root object as follows:

```
var node = search.findNode("workspace://SpacesStore/" + args.nodeid);
```

Here, we used the search root object and invoked the findNode() method of the JavaScript API for search root object. We are expecting nodeid to be passed as an argument; hence, we read it using args.nodeid. Before invoking the findNode() method for the node, we have to make the noderef string to be passed as an argument to the method; hence, we concatenated workspace://SpacesStore/ with nodeid. If a node is found, it will return a ScriptNode object representing the node found. If the node is not found, it will simply return null.

Checking user permissions on a node

Now, once the node is found, you first need to check whether a user has at least read access on the node or not before performing any other operations on a node as listed in the previous section. This can be done using the hasPermission method available in the ScriptNode API as follows:

```
var permission = node.hasPermission("Read");
```

We used the hasPermission() method from the ScriptNode API. We already had a node object available, and we just invoked the hasPermission() method passing the permission we want to check. If the current user has the given permission, it will return true. Otherwise, it will return false .

Getting the path of a node

As the next thing, you will be interested to get the path of the node in order to identify the folder hierarchy the node belongs to. You can easily get the display path of a node using the ScriptNode API as follows:

```
var nodepath = node.displayPath;
```

We accessed a variable displayPath from the ScriptNode class. There is already a getter method getDisplayPath() implemented to get the path of a node in the ScriptNode class. This method will return the display path for the given node.

Checking the properties of a node

Now, you want to see some properties of a node. For example, you are planning to modify the description property. Prior to this, you want to know what the value is before you change the value and want to log it for reference. The ScriptNode API is of biggest help when it comes to performing node-related things. With the help of the ScriptNode API, you can easily get the property value in different ways as follows:

```
var description = node.properties.description;
var description = node.properties["description"];
```

```
var description = node.properties["cm:description"];
var description = node.properties["{http://www.alfresco.org/model/
content/1.0}description"];
```

We just saw four different ways you can read the property of a node. If you have some custom property, you should use one of the last two options.

Logging the property value

Now before modifying the `description` property, you want to log the older value for reference. Using the `logger` root object, you can simply invoke the `log` method of the `logger` root object as follows:

```
logger.log("before change description value :" + description);
```

We used the `logger` root object and invoked the `log` method to log the property value. Each time logging is required to be added in the JavaScript controller, you can use the `logger.log()` method.

Modifying property of a node

Now, you want to modify the `description` property. Again with the help of the `ScriptNode` API, you can easily perform it as follows:

```
node.properties.description = "change in description";
```

We just set a new value to the `description` property. You can also use the other three ways we saw to access the property and set a new value for it.

Getting the current username and e-mail

You might be interested to know which user has invoked the web scripts. For this, you might want to log the username and e-mail address of the user who executed the web script as follows:

```
logger.log(person.properties.userName + " --- " + person.properties.
email + "--- executed webscript");
```

We used the root object `person`, which basically is `ScriptNode`. Also, we fetched the username and e-mail properties for a user who is currently running the web script. You can trace through the logs and find out which users executed the web script; this might be very useful at some point in time later.

Returning the guest home node

Let's say for some requirement, you need to get `noderef` of the guest home folder. This can be done using the `childByNamePath` method available in the `ScriptNode` API as follows:

```
model.foldernode = companyhome.childByNamePath("Guest Home");
```

In the response template, you can get the noderef value from the model object `foldernode` using the `TemplateNode` API the way we did in the earlier example.

We used the `companyhome` root object and the `childByNamePath()` method. For any `ScriptNode` type of object, you can use this method and get the `noderef` of its children. For example, you have a folder hierarchy `Company Home` > `Testing` > `QA` > `Performance_Testing`. Now if you have the node of `Testing` folder and you want to get the node of `Performance_Testing`, then you can call the method on the `Testing` folder node giving the path as `childByNamePath("QA/Performance_Testing")`.

Creating your own root object

We saw some of the generic examples of how to use root objects and JavaScript APIs in the JavaScript controller. You should be able to now explore the other root objects and related JavaScript APIs and find out which ones you can use to develop the web script as per your business requirement. Now, let's see something very interesting.

Consider a scenario wherein you want to execute some part of the JavaScript controller as a system user. The first thing that you will do is go through the available JavaScript APIs to find out whether there is a suitable API for this functionality is available or not. After doing an analysis, you will find that there isn't such an API available out-of-the-box. However, you found that if the web script had been a Java-backed web script, you could have used the Java API to do this. However, yours is the JavaScript-based web script. Now, what is next? You must be thinking how to perform this in the JavaScript API as well? No worries, it is possible to do the same in JavaScript controller as well. All you need to do is create a custom JavaScript extension.

Custom JavaScript extension

You learned earlier that each JavaScript API has `baseJavaScriptExtension` as a parent. You can try the following steps to create a custom JavaScript extension, which will provide you with the API methods to run some part of the web script as the system user and then revert back to the original user to execute the other portion of the web script:

1. Create a context file and add the following bean entry to it:

```
<bean id="customAdmin" parent="baseJavaScriptExtension"
  class="com.example.CustomAdminAPI">
  <property name="extensionName">
    <value>customauth</value>
  </property>
</bean>
```

2. Create a Java class `com.example.CustomAdminAPI`, which will extend the `org.alfresco.repo.processor.BaseProcessorExtension` class and declare the variable as follows:

```
net.sf.acegisecurity.Authentication auth;
```

3. Implement three public methods inside this class. The first method is to save current user's authentication, the second method is to run as a system user, and the third method is to clear the security context and set back the original user's authentication. The following is the code snippet for the three methods we just discussed:

```
public void saveCurrentUserAuthentication() {
  auth = AuthenticationUtil.getFullAuthentication();
}

public void executeAsSystemUser() {
  AuthenticationUtil.setRunAsUserSystem();
  AuthenticationUtil.setFullyAuthenticatedUser(AuthenticationUtil.
SYSTEM_USER_NAME);
}

public void setBackOriginalUserAuthentication() {
  AuthenticationUtil.clearCurrentSecurityContext();
  AuthenticationUtil.setFullAuthentication(this.auth);
}
```

4. Now, deploy the files and restart the server.

In your JavaScript-backed controller, you should now be using the newly created custom JavaScript extension as follows:

```
customauth.saveCurrentUserAuthentication();
customauth.executeAsSystemUser();
//Your piece of code you want to run as system user.
customauth.setBackOriginalUserAuthentication();
```

We just created a custom JavaScript extension, exposing a root object through which you can access the API methods created for it. This is how you can create a custom JavaScript extension in a scenario where you are not able to find the relevant API that you are looking for.

Summary

In this chapter, we have gone through all the possible functionalities that you can do inside your JavaScript controller for a web script using the available JavaScript APIs. We gained knowledge about how to identify the JavaScript APIs from the Alfresco codebase. We also went through the list of common root objects exposing the JavaScript APIs we found from the Alfresco codebase.

Next, we went through various other root objects provided by the web script framework in Alfresco. Later, we saw some code examples so you understand how to use root objects and the relevant JavaScript API inside the controller to do some generic operations on a node in Alfresco. At the end, you learned how to create a custom JavaScript extension to create your own root object and expose the relevant API method for the custom root object when the available JavaScript API does not meet your requirements. Overall, you have now got an understanding of how to develop a JavaScript controller using various JavaScript APIs to build up a web script controller as per your business requirements.

In the next chapter, we are going to take a look at some of the very useful and important things about web script development such as deploying, debugging, and troubleshooting web scripts.

8
Deployment, Debugging, and Troubleshooting Web Scripts

In this chapter, we will cover the following topics:

- Deployment options for Alfresco web scripts
- Details on debugging web scripts
- Useful troubleshooting pointers to some common problems related to web scripts
- Some important tips to execute web scripts on a production server

It is really important to know two things: how you can deploy what you have developed and how you can debug if something does not work the way it should. If you know these two things, then your job becomes easier and you can quickly identify the solution to some of the critical issues you are working on for your project.

While working on web scripts in Alfresco, the first phase of web script development is the creation of web scripts, wherein you will develop the required building blocks of a web script. The second most important phase is to deploy and register the web script in order to make the web script you have created available to the web script framework in Alfresco. This will enable you to make use of your web script. As a developer, it is important to understand various deployment options with which you can deploy Alfresco web scripts. Also, you should know how you can debug web scripts in Alfresco.

In this chapter, we will take a look at the possible ways you can deploy web scripts in Alfresco. Also, we will go through debugging techniques for web scripts and some useful troubleshooting pointers. We will also look at some useful tips that will be very helpful when executing web scripts for your project on a production server.

Deployment options

There are two possible ways you can have your web scripts deployed:

- Using the repository option
- Using the filesystem option

When creating web scripts in Alfresco, you might be creating Java-backed or JavaScript-backed web scripts for your project. Both can be deployed in different ways. It is important to know where you can deploy a web script with each deployment option and also which option is more suitable to you.

The repository option

In simple words, deploying a web script using the repository option means putting the web script component files inside a specific location within the repository.

First, let's take a look at the deployment of JavaScript-based web scripts. JavaScript-based web scripts can be deployed in the Alfresco repository. All the components for the JavaScript-based web script such as the description document, JavaScript-backed controller implementation, one or more response templates, configuration documents if any, and optional message bundles can be deployed in the Alfresco repository.

Now, for Java-backed web scripts, all the web script components except the controller implementation can be deployed in the Alfresco repository. In order to deploy web scripts using the repository option, it is necessary to know the location in the repository where we can place web scripts. A Java-backed controller cannot be deployed using the repository option.

The repository location where you can deploy web scripts is **Data Dictionary | Web Scripts Extensions**. If you create any new web scripts and choose to deploy them in the repository, then you must place all the required files in the mentioned location. Alfresco's out-of-the-box web scripts can be found at **Data Dictionary | Web Scripts**. As a general practice, you should always deploy your newly created custom web scripts under **Data Dictionary | Web Scripts Extensions** only.

Earlier, we created a JavaScript-based web script, hello world, and in order to deploy the web script we chose the repository option. We deployed all the relevant files for the hello world web script under **Web Scripts Extensions** in **Data Dictionary**.

The filesystem option

In simple words, deploying web scripts on the filesystem means putting the web script component files at a specific location inside your Alfresco installed directory. This deployment option can be used for both Java- and JavaScript-backed web scripts.

It is possible to deploy web scripts at the following locations:

- `tomcat\shared\classes\alfresco\extension\templates\webscripts`
- `tomcat\webapps\alfresco\WEB-INF\classes\alfresco\templates\webscripts`
- `tomcat\webapps\alfresco\WEB-INF\classes\alfresco\webscripts`
- `tomcat\webapps\alfresco\WEB-INF\classes\webscripts`

As a general practice, for new web scripts of your project, you should always use the first option and have web scripts deployed as Alfresco extensions. The second location mentioned previously is the one where you will find out-of-the-box web scripts provided by Alfresco. You might not find the last two locations mentioned previously inside your Alfresco installation directory. However, these are also places where you can deploy your web scripts. Ideally, you should not use these locations and use the first option.

Understanding deployment locations

We just saw that to deploy web scripts using the repository option, there are two probable locations where web scripts can be deployed. For deploying web scripts using the filesystem location, there are four such probable locations. As a developer, you must be interested to find out how these deployment locations are identified for both these deployment options.

It is good to know the technical details behind this. While registering web scripts, there is always a lookup of web scripts performed by the `org.springframework.` `extensions.webscripts.DeclarativeRegistry` class prior to registering the web script. It uses `org.springframework.extensions.webscripts.SearchPath`, which is basically a collection of `store`. If you take a look at each `store` defined under the `searchPath` collection, you will find the path locations, which are basically the six deployment locations we saw earlier. Let's take a look at how it is wired as a spring bean definition in Alfresco.

Here is the bean entry for `SearchPath` from `web-scripts-application-context.` `xml` that is available at the location `tomcat\webapps\alfresco\WEB-INF\classes\` `alfresco` inside your Alfresco installed directory. If you are using Alfresco Community 5, it is located under the `alfresco` package inside `alfresco-remote-` `api-*.jar`.

```
<bean id="webscripts.searchpath" class="org.springframework.
extensions.webscripts.SearchPath">
  <property name="searchPath">
    <list>
      <ref bean="webscripts.store.repo.extension" />
      <ref bean="webscripts.store.repo" />
      <ref bean="webscripts.store.client.extension" />
      <ref bean="webscripts.store.client" />
      <ref bean="webscripts.store.alfresco" />
      <ref bean="webscripts.store" />
    </list>
  </property>
</bean>
```

In the previous bean definition, under the `list` property, the first two beans are holding the path for repository deployment locations and the other four are holding the path for filesystem deployment locations we saw earlier. You can take a look at each of these bean definitions in `web-scripts-application-context.xml` for more details.

You must have some questions like what if the web script is deployed using both the repository and filesystem deployment options, or what will happen if a web script is deployed at more than one location, then which location would take precedence?

The answer to this is simple. Web scripts will be searched based on the order they have been displayed under the bean definition for SearchPath. This means that first it would search under the repository locations in sequence and then in the filesystem location in sequence.

Choosing the deployment option

Choosing the repository option or filesystem option for web script deployment can be decided based on a number of parameters, such as the number of web scripts to be developed for your project, whether frequent changes to the web scripts are required or not, whether the team members are given access to the server machines where Alfresco is installed, and whether you are looking to manage the code for web scripts as a part of your source control tree or not.

If a large number of web scripts are to be developed, then you should choose the filesystem deployment option and manage them as a part of your source control tree. The advantage of doing this will be that you can easily deploy web scripts that are building your business solutions along with your other customized extension code using the same build and deployment tool you used for customized extensions. There is no overhead of uploading web script files in the repository. You must also ensure that you have access to the server where Alfresco is installed; otherwise, you could be in trouble when you want to deploy and test the fixes you made to the web script and the fix quickly needs to be deployed on the live production system.

While using the repository option for deployment, web script files are present in the repository similar to other content. If you need to do some modification to your web scripts, then it can be easily done by editing the relevant file. Hence, web scripts can be easily edited when required. The good thing about this approach is that you do not need to have access to the server where Alfresco is installed. You just need to be able to access the repository through the user interface. In a scenario where some quick fixes are to be deployed to fix some critical issues, you can implement a JavaScript-based web script and deploy your web script using the repository option.

Debugging web scripts

You have completed the development of your web scripts, deployed them successfully, and even registered your web scripts to the web script engine. Now, while testing the web script functionalities, you found that the logic you have included in the web script controller is not working as expected. Hence, your web scripts are failing to return the required response. The next thing you want to find out is what went wrong and why they are not working the way they should. It's now time to debug to identify the issue that will give you hints to fix the issue. We will now take a look at how to enable logging, how to remote debug at the server, and also some useful debugging techniques.

Enable logging

Enabling the logging feature would be of great help while debugging an issue. Let's understand how to use logging in the case of both Java- and JavaScript-backed web scripts. The most important file you should remember is the `log4j.properties` file, which is available at the `tomcat\webapps\alfresco\WEB-INF\classes` location inside your Alfresco installation directory.

For debugging Java-backed web scripts, we need to perform the following steps:

1. You have the option to add `org.apache.log4j.Logger` statements in your Java implementation of the controller.

2. Then, you need to have the entry of your Java class added in the `log4j.properties` file.

3. For example, you have the Java class for your web script as `com.example.TestWebScript`. After adding the appropriate `logger` statements to the Java controller class, you should make an entry for the Java controller in the `log4j.properties` file as `log4j.logger.com.example.TestWebScript=debug`.

4. Restart the server and then hit your web script; you should be able to see the logger statements from the Java controller of the web script in the catalina logs.

For debugging JavaScript-backed web scripts, you will have to leverage the `logger` root object as follows:

1. You should add the required `logger` statements using the `logger.log` method in the JavaScript controller so that you can get enough details when you are looking at the logs.

2. To enable the logs to JavaScript-backed web scripts, you should set `log4j.logger.org.alfresco.repo.jscript` to debug and also `log4j.logger.org.alfresco.repo.jscript.ScriptLogger` to debug in `log4j.properties`.

3. Restart the server and then hit your web script; you should be able to see the `logger` statements from the JavaScript controller in the catalina logs.

Remote debugging on the server

Sometimes, only using the `logger` statements might not suffice to identify an issue, and you might also want to step through the code in order to find the issue. In such cases, you will need to do remote debugging of your code deployed on the server.

In order to be able to remote debug Java-backed web scripts, you should first set the following entry in the `catalina.bat` file in Windows and `catalina.sh` in Linux:

```
set DEBUG_OPTS=-Xdebug -Xrunjdwp:transport=dt_socket,server=y,suspend=n,address=8888
```

Then, restart the server. This will enable you to remote debug the Java code for your web script from your IDE such as Eclipse.

To debug the server-side JavaScript for your JavaScript-backed controller, you can use the Alfresco JavaScript debugger. You can enable the debugger in the following two ways:

1. In the `log4j.properties` file, set `log4j.logger.org.alfresco.repo.web.scripts.AlfrescoRhinoScriptDebugger` to on. This will display the debugger UI on the server startup. Also, set `log4j.logger.org.alfresco.repo.jscript.ScriptLogger=debug`.

2. Hit the debugger web script URL, `http://localhost:8080/alfresco/service/api/javascript/debugger`. It will display the **Enable** button on the screen. Click on it to open up the Alfresco JavaScript debugger UI.

It's very easy to debug through the JavaScript controller code using this debugger.

You just need to open the controller file by going to **File | Open**, and add the debug points to it. Now, hit the web script you want to debug.

The control will come to the debugger and you can now debug the code. There are options available such as **Step Into**, **Step Over**, or **Step Out** that will be helpful while debugging. Also, you can watch the value for the variables while debugging.

The following is a screenshot of the Alfresco JavaScript debugger user interface for your reference. To debug `share` web scripts, just replace `alfresco` with `share` in the previous URL.

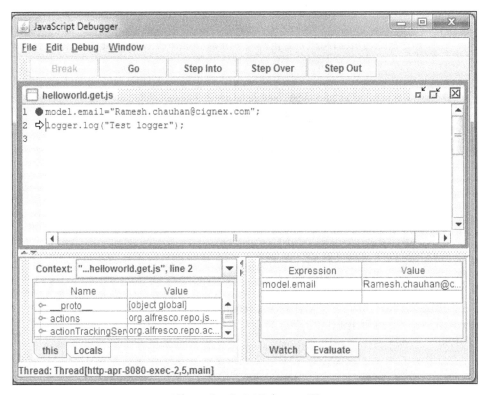

Alfresco JavaScript Debugger UI

The Alfresco JavaScript debugger can be accessed when Alfresco is running as a service or running from a console. To use this, you need to make sure that you are not running on a headless server, otherwise it will not display the debugger UI. Also, there may be possibilities that you might come across issues when trying to use the debugger UI when Alfresco is running as a service. Generally, you should use the debugger UI after starting your Alfresco server using the console instead of having Alfresco server started as a service. This will save a lot of your time, allowing you to focus on debugging your web-script-related issues instead of debugging through the issues of the debugger UI when the server started as a service.

Other debugging techniques

Let's take a look at some other debugging techniques that may be very useful:

- When your web script does not work, you should also check whether it is properly registered to the Alfresco web script engine or not. You can hit http://localhost:8080/alfresco/service/index and locate your web script from the various options available to browse web scripts, such as browse all by package or by URI. When you click on it, it will display the descriptor, JavaScript controller, and response template. You can make sure that the JavaScript controller has all your fixes or modifications that you added to fix the issue.

- In your web script, when you are working on some properties of a node, permissions on a node, and so on, you can also get help from nodebrowser. Using noderef, you can find out the details like properties set on the node, its children, aspects applied on it, associations with other nodes, and permissions on a node that might also be useful to you while debugging for your issue fix. You can also use other functionalities available in nodebrowser such as the ability to execute lucene queries that might also be helpful when you want to verify the lucene query used by the web script controller.

Troubleshooting pointers

Having understood the different ways to debug web scripts in Alfresco, let's take a look at some of the troubleshooting pointers for some common issues you might come across while working with Alfresco web scripts.

A valid SecureContext error

You might have sometimes faced the error **A valid SecureContext was not provided in the RequestContext**. There can be many reasons for getting this error. Some of them are listed as follows:

- When you have set authentication to none in the web script description document, and in the controller you are trying to invoke some public services of Alfresco that require authentication, for example, calling the toDisplayPath() method, it will give you the mentioned exception.

- If you have a JavaScript-backed controller for your web script and you have deployed it using the repository option and authentication is set to none, you will get the mentioned exception when you try to hit your web script.

> If you are deploying a JavaScript-backed web script using the repository option, make sure that the web script has the authentication level set and it should not be set as none.

Web Script format " is not registered

While developing web scripts in Alfresco, you might have come across an error **Web Script format " is not registered** when you tried hitting the web script.

The reason is that if you have a JavaScript-backed controller or Java controller extending the `DeclarativeWebScript` class, and in your web script's description document you have a default format specified as blank such as `<format default="">`, then this error will appear.

> When you want to take control to return the response without a template, you should use the Java-backed controller extending the `AbstractWebScript` class. In this case, having specified the default format as blank in the web script description document will not cause the mentioned error.

Cannot locate template processor for template

For your web script, you have created a description document, required controller implementation, and required response template. Now, when you try to execute the web script, you get the error **Cannot locate template processor for template example/contentlocation.get.xml**.

Looking at the error, you will first think that you already have the template in place, so why does this error occur? It is sometimes really tricky to find out what the issue is. The same is the case here. The reason for this error is that the name of the template is not as per the web script naming convention. It should be `contentlocation.get.xml.ftl` instead of `contentlocation.get.xml`.

> You must always ensure that you adhere to the web script naming convention and always deploy the web script files at correct locations. If you have a Java-backed controller, make sure that the bean ID for Java-backed controller is specified as expected.

Script URL does not support the method

In simple words, this error generally occurs when you do not use the appropriate method to invoke the web script. For example, when you have a POST web script and you invoke the web script as a GET request, you will see the script URL does not support the method error. In order to avoid this error, you should always use the appropriate method to invoke the web scripts.

Web scripts on a production server

A production server sounds interesting, doesn't it? Yes, this is the most important thing. While working on live projects and supporting a production system with Alfresco as a backend repository for your client, you might have to write different web scripts as per the business requirement. This might take longer to execute as the production server will be dealing with a large number of content as compared to your development servers. For example, you might have to write a patch script to add an extra property on existing nodes, or you might need to write a web script to retrieve records for some specific criteria. Let's take a look at what you should take care of while running such web scripts on a production server.

Running web scripts in the background

It might be possible that the web script that you have written once executed against a large number of content might take longer to process. In such cases, you cannot hit the web script from a browser and keep on waiting until the response is received. For such web scripts, when required to run on the production server, one approach you can choose is to run the web script in the background and invoke the web script directly from the server itself so that you need not have to worry about the calling client getting disconnected from the server.

In order to be able to run web scripts in the background, one way is to invoke the web script from a shell script. You can then run the shell script in the background from the server itself. You can use the following example command to run the shell script in the background:

```
nohup execute-webscript.sh > webscript.log &
```

This command will run `execute-webscript.sh` in the background, which is basically your shell script invoking your web script, and will dump the execution logs of the shell script to the `webscript.log` file. You might probably also want to implement an e-mail notification feature to trigger an e-mail once the web script execution is completed so that you do not have to monitor the logs frequently and can get a notification once the web script execution is completed.

Logging web script logs separately

Let's take a look at another important thing that could be very useful. While executing long running web scripts with a Java-backed controller, you might have added some important debug statements in your web scripts to capture some important details on execution, and as the web scripts will be running in the background, they will keep on adding the logs. As it is the production server, the other logs from the application must be continuously added to catalina.out. Now, if you don't separate out the logs for your patch web script, then it would be really difficult for you to find out the required details about the logs added by your web script from catalina.out. So, you might be interested to have your web script add logs to a separate logfile. This will make it easier for you if you want to go through the logs for your web script's execution. This can be done by adding the following entry in the log4j.properties file:

```
log4j.logger.packagename_of_Javaclass_for_webscript=debug, wsappender
log4j.additivity.packagename_of_Javaclass_for_webscript=false

log4j.appender.wsappender=org.apache.log4j.DailyRollingFileAppender
log4j.appender.wsappender.File=location_to_log_file_with_filename
log4j.appender.wsappender.DatePattern='.'yyyy-MM-dd
log4j.appender.wsappender.layout=org.apache.log4j.PatternLayout
log4j.appender.wsappender.layout.ConversionPattern=%d{ABSOLUTE} %-5p
[%c] %m%n
```

In the previous entry, you will have to provide the package name of the Java controller class for your web script at the places highlighted. Then, provide the location where you want to place the logfile and also give the name of the logfile along with the location.

Disabling Java-backed web scripts

We know that for the JavaScript-backed web script, web script files can be directly deployed either on the filesystem or in the repository. To add or remove a JavaScript-backed web script, server restart is not needed. We just need to refresh web scripts by hitting the http://localhost:8080/alfresco/service/index URL. Hence, in a scenario where on the production system you want to disable some JavaScript-backed web scripts, you can easily do so without a server restart.

Now, you must be thinking what if you have to disable a Java-backed web script on the production server? You might also be thinking that, as there will be a bean entry for the Java-backed web script in a Spring context file as per the naming convention to map that bean as a controller for a web script, how is it possible to disable the Java-backed web script without restarting the server? It is possible to disable Java-backed web scripts as well on the running server. In order to disable Java-backed web scripts without server restart, you should just simply remove or rename the description file and response templates for the web script. For example, make the description file and response template as `*.bak`. Then, just refresh the web scripts hitting the URL `http://localhost:8080/alfresco/service/index`. Now, the web script is disabled and you will not be able to access it.

Summary

In this chapter, we have gone through the possible deployment options for web scripts in Alfresco and got an understanding of how the web script framework in Alfresco decides the precedence for the web scripts when deployed at multiple locations. We also looked at some of the factors that will help you choose the deployment option as required. We also looked at how to debug web scripts to find out what went wrong with your web script. We have also gone through troubleshooting pointers for some of the common issues you might face while working on web scripts. At the end, we went through some useful tips and tricks that might be helpful when you are running web scripts on a production server. Overall, now you have a good understanding of how to deploy and debug the web scripts in Alfresco, and the next time when you need to run some web scripts on a production server, you will have some ideas to share with peer developers or the project manager about how you can approach executing web scripts on a production server.

Now, when you need to develop a large number of web scripts, you cannot have them developed without having a project structure as you will be working in a team, and at the end of the day, all your code should be available in the source control tree. It's important to set up the development project to develop web scripts. In the next chapter, we are going to take a look at how to set up a development project in Eclipse that can be built using Maven build.

9
Mavenizing Web Scripts

In this chapter, we will cover the following topics:

- Setting up a development environment with Maven
- Creating the default project structure with the Alfresco Maven SDK
- Building an **Alfresco Module Package** (**AMP**) with Maven
- Setting up a development environment in Eclipse
- Understanding the default project structure
- Extending the default project structure to create web scripts
- Applying the AMP to the Alfresco WAR using Maven in order to test the developed web scripts locally
- Things to know about using Maven with Alfresco enterprise version

So far, in our exploration of Alfresco web scripts, we have gained an understanding of how to develop web scripts and deploy them. We did not use any project structure for the web scripts we developed in the previous chapters; also, we did not use any tool to build web scripts. We simply created the required files for the web script in an editor of our choice and then manually deployed web script files to the filesystem locations. It was feasible to do this as there were fewer web scripts and we were doing it to understand web scripts. However, consider a scenario where you have to develop a large number of web scripts for your project. In such a scenario, it would not be a suitable option to independently create web script files and deploy them manually. In this case, you definitely need to follow a project structure for the development of web scripts. Also, you need to have a mechanism for the deployment of web scripts so that you can deploy all the web scripts on the server easily and effectively without manually transferring the web script files.

Now, you might have a few questions, such as how can I set up a project structure to develop web scripts? What kind of deployment artifacts can be used to deploy web scripts in Alfresco? What tool can be used to build the required deployment artifacts? What prerequisites should be considered and kept ready before using the tool? Do I need to have detailed knowledge about the tool? How will I proceed about it?

Do not worry about all these questions. We are going to find solutions to them in this chapter.

Let's first briefly cover the answers to the previous questions. You should create a project using Alfresco Maven SDK that is basically a community project also supported by Alfresco, which provides a very easy-to-use approach to create extensions for Alfresco. You should use **Alfresco Module Package** (**AMP**) as the deployment artifact. An AMP is basically a ZIP file with a specific folder structure that includes all the required files you have developed for your alfresco project. Generally, an AMP file will be applied to the vanilla Alfresco WAR file using **module management tool** when deploying on the required server. You can use Apache Maven to build the AMP file as the required deployment artifact. Apache Maven is basically a build management tool that will understand the JAR dependencies of the project and will retrieve them.

It is okay if you are not familiar with Maven and do not have knowledge about it. We are not going to explore Alfresco Maven SDK, AMP, and Maven in this chapter. We have already covered a basic overview of what they are and this is enough for now to get started. Our main goal in this chapter is to get a basic understanding of how you can use Alfresco Maven SDK to create a defined project structure, have the project available in Eclipse, and build the AMP as deployment artifact for your web scripts development and also how to apply AMP to out-of-the-box Alfresco WAR using Maven to test the functionalities.

Setting up your environment

Before we start, it is important to understand that Alfresco Maven SDK is compatible with Alfresco Community Versions 4.2 and above, and Alfresco Enterprise Versions 4.1.2 and above. It is interesting to know that, while using the Alfresco Maven SDK, you do not need to have Alfresco installed on your machine manually. The Alfresco Maven SDK will make the job easier for you and it will take care of downloading Alfresco on your machine based on the entries provided for version and `groupId` in the **Project Object Model (POM)** XML for your project.

Now, let's first make sure that we have the required prerequisites in place on our development machine before we begin creating a project using Alfresco Maven SDK:

- You need to have JDK 1.7 installed on your machine and configured properly. **Java Development Kit (JDK)** is basically a development environment to build applications using the Java programming language. You can download this from `http://www.oracle.com/technetwork/java/javase/downloads/jdk7-downloads-1880260.html`. Once downloaded and installed, make sure to set up the `JAVA_HOME` environment variable and also the **Path** variable.

- You need to have Apache Maven 3.0.3 or above installed and configured properly. You can download this from `http://maven.apache.org/download.cgi`. You will also find the required instructions to install it based on the operating system you are using. Once downloaded and installed successfully, make sure that the environment variable `M2E_HOME` is set correctly and also the **Path** variable is modified accordingly.

Now, let's check whether Maven is referring to the correct JDK installation and ensure that you have installed the correct version of Maven by running the `mvn -version` command. On a Windows machine, running this command from the command prompt will display information about the Maven version, Maven home, Java version used by Maven, and the Java home:

```
C:\Users\ramesh.chauhan>mvn -version
Apache Maven 3.0.4 (r1232337; 2012-01-17 14:14:56+0530)
Maven home: D:\apache-maven-3.0.4\bin\..
Java version: 1.7.0_51, vendor: Oracle Corporation
Java home: C:\Program Files\Java\jdk1.7.0_51\jre
Default locale: en_US, platform encoding: Cp1252
OS name: "windows 7", version: "6.1", arch: "amd64", family: "windows"
```

Exploring the Alfresco Maven repository

The Alfresco Maven repository is basically a common location where all the dependency JARs related to Alfresco are kept available, and you can configure your project to refer to the required dependencies from the repository in the `pom.xml` file of the project. You might want to explore the Maven repository for Alfresco that will be used by the Alfresco Maven SDK. Visit `https://artifacts.alfresco.com/nexus/#view-repositories` and explore the public release repositories that contain the released and stable artifacts. Also, the different available default project templates that are known as archetype in the terminology of Maven can be found under archetype-catalog available at `https://artifacts.alfresco.com/nexus/service/local/repo_groups/public/content/archetype-catalog.xml`.

Creating the default project structure for AMP

In order to create the project structure for an AMP, we will use the project template provided by the Alfresco Maven SDK. This default project template is basically known as **AMP archetype**. This project template helps to have a standardized development, deployment, and the release approach for the Alfresco extensions you will develop for your project. The Alfresco AMP archetype can be used to create both repositories as well as share AMPs when required. In this chapter, we are going to use the AMP archetype for repository web scripts.

> The Alfresco Maven SDK also provides another useful archetype known as All-in-One archetype, which is basically a multi-module project and gives a complete installation of the Alfresco platform along with its components without requiring additional downloads. While exploring `archetype-catalog.xml`, you might have observed that there are a lot of archetypes available. The important archetypes, the Alfresco AMP archetype and All-in-One archetype can be identified having the `org.alfresco.maven.archetype` group ID in `archetype-catalog.xml`.

In order to create a default AMP project using the Alfresco AMP archetype, perform the following steps:

1. Run the following command from the console. Just to note here, if the `https` link does not work for you, then you can try using `http` instead of `https` in the following code snippet:

   ```
   mvn archetype:generate -DarchetypeCatalog=https://artifacts.
   alfresco.com/nexus/content/groups/public/archetype-catalog.xml
   -Dfilter=org.alfresco.maven.archetype:
   ```

```
C:\Users\ramesh.chauhan>mvn archetype:generate -DarchetypeCatalog=https://artifacts.alfresco.com/nex
us/content/groups/public/archetype-catalog.xml -Dfilter=org.alfresco.maven.archetype:
[INFO] Scanning for projects...
[INFO]
[INFO] ------------------------------------------------------------------------
[INFO] Building Maven Stub Project (No POM) 1
[INFO]
[INFO] ------------------------------------------------------------------------
[INFO]
[INFO] >>> maven-archetype-plugin:2.2:generate (default-cli) @ standalone-pom >>>
[INFO]
[INFO] <<< maven-archetype-plugin:2.2:generate (default-cli) @ standalone-pom <<<
[INFO]
[INFO] --- maven-archetype-plugin:2.2:generate (default-cli) @ standalone-pom ---
[INFO] Generating project in Interactive mode
[INFO] No archetype defined. Using maven-archetype-quickstart (org.apache.maven.archetypes:maven-arc
hetype-quickstart:1.0)
```

2. You will be displayed with the available archetypes along with brief details about them, as shown in the following screenshot. You will be prompted to select an archetype. Type 1 and press *Enter*, as shown in the following screenshot:

```
Choose archetype:
1: https://artifacts.alfresco.com/nexus/content/groups/public/archetype-catalog.xml -> org.alfresco.
maven.archetype:alfresco-amp-archetype (Sample project with full support for lifecycle and rapid dev
elopment of AMPs (Alfresco Module Packages))
2: https://artifacts.alfresco.com/nexus/content/groups/public/archetype-catalog.xml -> org.alfresco.
maven.archetype:alfresco-allinone-archetype (Sample multi-module project for All-in-One development
on the Alfresco platform. Includes modules for: Repository, AMP, Share, Solr, Web Quick Start and em
bedded Jetty run)
Choose a number or apply filter (format: [groupId:]artifactId, case sensitive contains): : 1
```

3. In the next step, you will be asked to select the version of the archetype to have as a base for your project. This will list the available versions for the archetype you have selected. You can find these versions from the `archetype-catalog.xml` file as well. For the AMP archetype, 1.1.1 is the latest version at present. So, Type 5 and press *Enter*, as shown in the following screenshot:

```
Choose org.alfresco.maven.archetype:alfresco-amp-archetype version:
1: 1.0
2: 1.0.1
3: 1.0.2
4: 1.1.0
5: 1.1.1
Choose a number: 5: 5
```

4. Next, you will be prompted to provide the value for `groupId`, which you can consider as a package name in the terminology of Java. You can provide any name you like suitable for your project. Here, we will provide `com.example` as `groupId`, as shown in the following code:

```
Define value for property 'groupId': : com.example
```

5. Now, you will be prompted to provide the value for artifactId, which is basically the name of your project and also the name of the AMP file that we will be generating as a deployment package for the project. So, give a meaningful unique name as per your project. Generally, as a good practice, you might want to append repo to AMP file name to indicate that AMP will contain repository-related extensions. Here, we will provide example-repo as artifactId, as shown in the following code:

Define value for property 'artifactId': : example-repo

6. You will now see a summary with the values you entered and some of the default values such as the target version of Alfresco. If you find the details appropriate, then type Y and press *Enter*. If you want to change the details, type N and press *Enter*. It would then ask you to reenter the details. Here, we will type Y and press *Enter* as follows:

```
[INFO] Using property: version = 1.0-SNAPSHOT
[INFO] Using property: package = (not used)
[INFO] Using property: alfresco_target_amp_client_war = alfresco
[INFO] Using property: alfresco_target_amp_client_war_groupId = org.alfresco
[INFO] Using property: alfresco_target_amp_client_war_version = 4.2.e
[INFO] Using property: alfresco_target_groupId = org.alfresco
[INFO] Using property: alfresco_target_version = 4.2.e
Confirm properties configuration:
groupId: com.example
artifactId: example-repo
version: 1.0-SNAPSHOT
package: (not used)
alfresco_target_amp_client_war: alfresco
alfresco_target_amp_client_war_groupId: org.alfresco
alfresco_target_amp_client_war_version: 4.2.e
alfresco_target_groupId: org.alfresco
alfresco_target_version: 4.2.e
Y: : Y_
```

If you are interested to find out how the value for Alfresco version 4.2.e was shown as defaulted value, then here is how you can find it out. You first need to take a look at archetype-catalog.xml and then find the entry for the artifcatId: alfresco-amp-archetype. Now, hit the URL mentioned under the repository tag and traverse as per the package name specified in groupId, that is, org.alfresco.maven. archetype and click on alfresco-amp-archetype, click on 1.1.1, and download alfresco-amp-archetype-1.1.1.jar. The URL will look like this: https://artifacts.alfresco.com/nexus/ content/groups/public/org/alfresco/maven/archetype/ alfresco-amp-archetype/1.1.1/. If you take a look inside the JAR, under META-INF/maven/archetype-metadata.xml, you can find the value as 4.2.e defaulted.

7. Now, after some processing by Maven, it will display the **BUILD SUCCESS** message on the console and display the location of the project created from the archetype as an informational message, as shown in the following screenshot:

```
[INFO] ------------------------------------------------------------------------
[INFO] Using following parameters for creating project from Archetype: alfresco-amp-archetype:1.1.1
[INFO] ------------------------------------------------------------------------
[INFO] Parameter: groupId, Value: com.example
[INFO] Parameter: artifactId, Value: example-repo
[INFO] Parameter: version, Value: 1.0-SNAPSHOT
[INFO] Parameter: package, Value: (not used)
[INFO] Parameter: packageInPathFormat, Value: (not used)
[INFO] Parameter: alfresco_target_amp_client_war, Value: alfresco
[INFO] Parameter: groupId, Value: com.example
[INFO] Parameter: version, Value: 1.0-SNAPSHOT
[INFO] Parameter: alfresco_target_groupId, Value: org.alfresco
[INFO] Parameter: alfresco_target_amp_client_war_groupId, Value: org.alfresco
[INFO] Parameter: package, Value: (not used)
[INFO] Parameter: alfresco_target_version, Value: 4.2.e
[INFO] Parameter: artifactId, Value: example-repo
[INFO] Parameter: alfresco_target_amp_client_war_version, Value: 4.2.e
[INFO] project created from Archetype in dir: C:\Users\ramesh.chauhan\example-repo
[INFO] ------------------------------------------------------------------------
[INFO] BUILD SUCCESS
[INFO] ------------------------------------------------------------------------
[INFO] Total time: 30.296s
[INFO] Finished at: Fri Aug 15 18:00:40 IST 2014
[INFO] Final Memory: 16M/152M
[INFO] ------------------------------------------------------------------------
```

It has generated a sample project structure for the Alfresco project as required to generate an AMP file. You can now go to the location where the default project structure has been created and explore it. Here project structure was created at the location C:\Users\ramesh.chauhan\example-repo. Inside the generated project structure, the most important file that you will find is pom.xml that is basically used for every Maven project to indicate to Maven about the project dependencies. Along with pom.xml, the generated project structure also contains the default configuration files and sample Java code with its supporting unit test and the configuration to run a local Alfresco instance for testing.

Generating AMP from the default project

Once the default project structure is ready, let's try to generate the AMP file for it. Go to the location of the created project structure. In order to create an AMP file for it, run the mvn package -DskipTests=true command.

Here, we are not interested in running the tests while generating the AMP; hence, we have explicitly mentioned skipTests as true. If you want to run the test as well, you should simply execute the mvn package command.

Running the preceding command should create an AMP file named `example-repo.amp` under the target folder inside the project we created. You can open the AMP file with any ZIP extractor and browse through it.

 You can use the default project structure to not only create web scripts, but also for other customizations to Alfresco such as custom actions, custom content model, custom workflow, and so on, and create an AMP to make them deployment ready.

Now, run the `mvn clean` command that will just clean up the target folder. Hence, the generated AMP file will also be removed. We did this purposefully as we want to come back to the default project structure and import the project structure in Eclipse. Also, we want to gain an understanding of the files and directories present in the default project structure.

Setting up a development environment with Eclipse

At this stage, the project structure created from archetype made available by the Alfresco Maven SDK is ready on the filesystem. Now, in the next step, we want to have the same project structure available in Eclipse so that we can start with the development of the web scripts from the Eclipse IDE with the defined project structure. You can download the Eclipse IDE from different release packages available on `http://www.eclipse.org/downloads/packages/` as per the operating system you are using. Just make sure that it supports Maven plugins.

 In this chapter, we will use the Eclipse Java EE IDE from Luna packages that come with built-in Maven support. You might use another version of Eclipse version, so you need to make sure that if it does not have built-in Maven support, the Maven plugins for Eclipse IDE are added. Adding Maven plugin to the Eclipse IDE is a simple process and you should be able to do it easily.

Now, in order to import the default project structure to Eclipse, perform the following steps:

1. Open the Eclipse IDE. Click on **File** | **Import** | **Maven** | **Existing Maven Projects** and click on **Next**.

2. In the screen displayed, navigate to the project location on the local filesystem and click on **OK**. It should then display a selected checkbox against **pom.xml** for the project. Then, click on **Finish**.

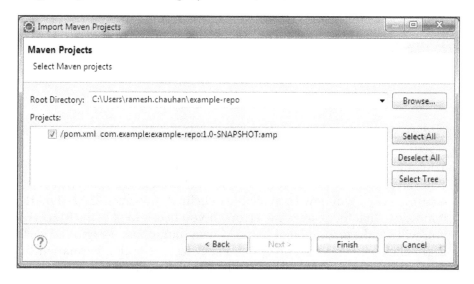

3. On the next screen, an error for the Alfresco Maven plugin **set-version** will be displayed, as shown in the following screenshot. Ignore the error for now and click on **Finish**.

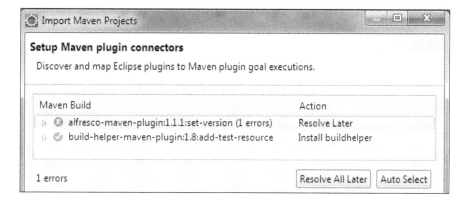

4. A **Incomplete Maven Goal Execution** pop up will then be displayed, as shown in the following screenshot. Click on **OK**.

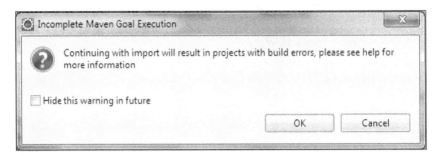

5. You might then see a window asking you to install a build helper plugin. You can proceed with it if you want, or, just click on Cancel. The Project `example-repo` will now be available in Eclipse; however, the red mark on it indicates that there are some errors. If you take a look at the **Markers** tab, you will see the error related to the Maven plugin that we ignored earlier. Right-click on it and click on **Quick Fix**. Select the option **Permanently mark goal set-version in pom.xml as ignored in Eclipse build**. It will display the option to select the POM location. Select the POM location and click on **OK**.

6. Now, right-click on the **example-repo** project. Go to **Maven | Update project** and click on **OK**. The project has now been successfully imported, and there are no errors except warning messages for unused imports for the Java classes present in the default package. You can ignore them.

 While importing a project in the Eclipse for the first time, if you have any build path-related errors, then make sure you update the project as we did in the last step and ensure that all the Maven dependencies have been downloaded on your local machine.

Now, we have the default project structure imported in the Eclipse IDE as a Maven project.

Understanding the default project structure

Having imported the project in Eclipse, let's now go through the project structure in order to understand the important files and directories present in it:

File/directory in project structure	Brief description
`pom.xml`	For any Maven project, `pom.xml` is a must in order to let Maven know about the project dependencies. The `pom.xml` file is available directly under the project directory. If you take a look at `pom.xml`, you will get all the details about the project dependencies, repository information, and other important information. Also, in `pom.xml` for our project, you should be able to see the settings we provided while generating the project from the Maven archetype. You can change them here if you want and just update the project as we did earlier. Maven would then consider the updated changes and take care of the required things.
`src/main/java`	This directory will be used for placing the Java source code for the project. You can organize Java classes under the appropriate package under this location. The Java controller for web scripts you will be developing for your project should be placed under this location. Apart from web script controllers, you can also place Java classes for other customizations such as custom actions and others. When the project is built, Java classes placed here will be available in a JAR file inside the AMP generated as a deployment artifact. When the AMP is applied to the Alfresco WAR file, the JAR file will be deployed under `WEB-INF/lib`.
`src/main/amp`	All the required details related to AMP reside under this location. The `module.properties` file is an important file for the AMP structure. It contains details about the AMP file such as ID for AMP, version, dependencies, and minimum and maximum version of Alfresco to run it. The location `src/main/amp/config/alfresco/module/example-repo` is the core of AMP and will contain important files such as Spring configuration context files, content model files, and so on. You can create extensions, messages folder under `src/main/amp/config/alfresco` in order to include the web script component files.
`src/test`	The unit test cases-related implementation and the supporting configuration that run the unit test cases will be placed here. Just take a look at the default folders available under this location and you will get an understanding of what is present inside the default folders.

Extending your default project to create web scripts

While developing web scripts in the previous chapters, we did not follow any project structure and developed the required files for a web script independently in an editor of our choice and then manually deployed them at the appropriate locations in the installed Alfresco directory. Now, having understood the project structure and the AMP deployment package, it is time to discover how we can extend the default project structure in order to create web scripts. Let's try to understand where you should place the web script-related files in the project structure while developing new web scripts:

- The web script descriptor file (*.desc.xml), response templates for the web script (*.ftl), configuration document for the web script (*.config.xml), and message bundles (*.properties) should be placed under the location src/main/amp. Inside the default structure available in src/main/amp/config/alfresco, create a new folder structure, /extension/templates/webscripts, to store all the new web scripts you will create. You can then classify the web scripts in different packages inside this location, for example, all the login related customized web script and its descriptor, response template, configuration document, and message bundle can be placed under location src/main/amp/config/alfresco/extension/templates/webscripts/login.

- For JavaScript-based web scripts, the controller implementation (*.js) should also be placed at the same location along with other files as mentioned in the previous point.

- For Java-backed web scripts, the controller implementation (*.java) should be placed under the appropriate package structure inside src/main/java.

- For Java-backed web script, the Spring configuration context file that associates controller with the web script should be placed under src/main/amp/config/alfresco/extension. You can also place your Spring bean mapping entry from your Java controller inside the module-context.xml file under src/main/amp/config/alfresco/module/proj-name.

 Once you generate the AMP for the project running the Maven package, you should be able to see that all the Java classes are put into a JAR file, whereas other files are appropriately located in the AMP file as we placed them under the project structure. You can now give this AMP file for deployment to other server.

Applying AMP to the Alfresco WAR for testing

Once you are done with the web script development for your project following the preceding project structure, create an AMP file for your project and test it before you hand over the AMP file for deployment on the other server. In order to test your web scripts locally, you will first need to apply the AMP to the Alfresco WAR file. With the Alfresco Maven SDK, you need not have Alfresco installed locally for applying the AMP. From the console, you can just go inside the project's location and simply execute the `mvn integration-test -Pamp-to-war` command.

After running the preceding command, you will be able to see that Maven is now doing its job to download all the required dependencies to compile the project. This will create an AMP file for the project, apply the AMP file to the out-of-the-box Alfresco WAR, and then deploy the WAR to the embedded Tomcat server, and finally, start the server. You should be able to see from the console output that the AMP module for your project has been successfully generated and known to the Alfresco server.

You can log in to the Alfresco server `http://localhost:8080/alfresco` and also hit the web script URLs for the web scripts you have developed. Once you are done with testing, make sure you shut down the running server. You can simply press *Ctrl + C* on the console from where you ran the Maven integration command to shut the server down.

> If you get an out-of-memory error while running the previous integration test command, you will need to increase the size of the memory allocated to Alfresco and Tomcat. You can do this by providing Maven with additional JVM memory settings such as increasing PermGen size.

We have just seen that without having Alfresco installed previously on the development machine, we were able to test our customized development very easily with the help of the Alfresco Maven SDK. All we have done is just executed a command, and Maven did everything required for us and made the job easier, leaving us to focus more on development and not worry about things such as downloading and setting up Alfresco on the local machine, generating AMP, and deploying it to the Alfresco WAR.

If you are using Alfresco enterprise version and want to use Maven, then you first need to have the valid credentials to access the Alfresco private repository. You will need to get in touch with the Alfresco support team at `https://myalfresco.force.com/support` to get the credential details to access the Alfresco private repository and incorporate the suggested Maven configurations to access the Alfresco private repository.

Summary

In this chapter, we have gained a basic understanding of how you can make your Alfresco web script development and deployment experience easy with Maven support provided by the Alfresco Maven SDK. First, we went through setting prerequisites to set up the development environment with Maven. We gained knowledge about how to create the default project structure in order to create the Alfresco deployment package as AMP, and then we understood how to generate AMP for the default project structure. Later, we imported the project into the Eclipse IDE and set up the development environment and then gained knowledge about the various files and directories present in the default project structure.

We then looked at how you can extend the default project structure to develop JavaScript- and Java-based web scripts for your project. Also, we learned how to apply AMP to Alfresco WAR using the Maven command to test the developed functionality locally without having Alfresco installed on the local machine. At the end, we went through what you should do in order to use Maven with your enterprise version of Alfresco. Overall, you now have a basic understanding in order to get going with Alfresco web script development using Maven support.

In the next chapter, we are going to take a look at how you can extend the web script framework in Alfresco.

10
Extending the Web Script Framework

In this chapter, we will cover:

- Extending the web script runtime to create a custom implementation
- Customized implementation of a web script container
- Adding your own authenticator implementation to the web script framework
- Script processor and template processor custom implementation
- Customizing formats

We started our journey of learning Alfresco web scripts by getting familiar with web scripts. We then did a hands-on exercise to create our first web script in Alfresco and gained in-depth technical knowledge on understanding the web script framework in Alfresco in and out. Later, we got well acquainted with the building blocks of web scripts and different ways to invoke web scripts. We also understood how to create Java-backed web scripts and then explored JavaScript-based web scripts in detail. Next, we looked into the deployment, debugging, and troubleshooting of web scripts, and then we learned how to set up the development environment with Maven. By now, you should have gained the required knowledge to practically implement and use Alfresco web scripts in your live projects. Also, you should be able to debug, troubleshoot, and fix issues with web scripts in your project. Now, as the last thing to learn in this book, it's time to find out about the possibilities to extend the web script framework in Alfresco.

Before we start, you might want to refresh your knowledge on the web script framework that we learned about in *Chapter 3, Understanding the Web Script Framework*. As a brief summary, the core components of the web script framework are web script runtime, web script container, and authenticator. Other supporting components of the web script container are the script processor registry to register the script processors, the template processor registry to register the template processors, and the format registry to register new formats. We have gone through the details of out-of-the-box implementation classes for all of them. The web script framework in Alfresco is very powerful and the out-of-the-box implementation provided for the core components of the web script framework caters to all your needs related to web scripts implementation for your project. However, in order to understand how powerful the web script framework in Alfresco is, it is worth taking a look at how you can extend the web script framework's core components and add your customized implementation for it. In general scenarios, you will not be required to make any changes to the web script framework's components. However, having knowledge about the possibility to extend the web script framework will help you to have a customized implementation if required. It will also get you familiar with the power of working on open source implementations, which provides the flexibility to add your customized implementation whenever required.

We are going to take a look at how it is possible to extend the web script framework in Alfresco to have custom implementation of web script runtime, web script container, authenticators, script processors and template processors, and also custom formats.

Custom implementation of the web script runtime

Let's first briefly understand the role of the web script runtime in the web script framework. During the web script execution flow, once the request dispatcher sends the request, the web script runtime will delegate the request to the web script container for further processing in order to execute the web script. There are different implementations available for the web script runtime such as servlet runtime, portlet runtime, JSF runtime, Facebook runtime, and SURF web framework runtime. As a developer, you must be interested in knowing what needs to be done if a new implementation for the web script runtime is to be implemented. Let's take a look at it here.

In order to understand how to create a customized implementation of the web script runtime in the web script framework, first let's take a look at the service provider interface provided by the web script framework, which opens up the possibilities to create custom implementation. If you take a look at the implementation inside `spring-webscripts-*.jar`, there is an interface defined, `org.springframework.extensions.webscripts.Runtime`, which declares the required methods to be implemented by any web script runtime. In order to make a simplified implementation, there is an abstract class implementation, `org.springframework.extensions.webscripts.AbstractRuntime`, which implements the `org.springframework.extensions.webscripts.Runtime` interface. This provides the implementation for the methods defined in the interface in a way that any runtime in the web script framework should be able to serve a web script request in a generic way. The `AbstractRuntime` class leaves some of the methods as abstract leaving the child class to provide the implementation for the abstract methods in order to make a generic implementation for the web script runtime. If you take a look at all the existing web script runtimes available in the web script framework, such as `WebScriptServletRuntime` and `JSFRuntime`, you can see that they extend from the `AbstractRuntime` class. These classes provide the implementation of the required abstract methods from the `AbstractRuntime` class.

Having an overall understanding about the service provider interface and its implementation in the out-of-the-box web script framework in Alfresco, let's try to understand how we can use this knowledge to create a custom implementation of the web script runtime. We are going to take a look at the high level steps required to create a custom web script runtime.

In order to create a custom web script runtime, perform the following steps:

1. Open Eclipse and inside your project, create a Java class that extends `org.springframework.extensions.webscripts.AbstractRuntime`.

2. You will see that Eclipse displays red symbol at the class declaration. Do not worry about this. This happens because we have not yet provided the implementation for the abstract methods provided in the parent class. Right-click on the class and go to **Source | Override/Implement Methods** and click on **OK**. You should be able to see the default implementation for the abstract methods from the `AbstractRuntime` parent class. The following are the methods you will be required to provide an implementation for to create a custom web script runtime:

   ```
   public String getName()
   protected String getScriptMethod()
   protected String getScriptUrl()
   protected WebScriptRequest createRequest(Match paramMatch)
   protected WebScriptResponse createResponse()
   protected Authenticator createAuthenticator()
   protected WebScriptSessionFactory createSessionFactory()
   ```

3. You will also be required to provide an explicit constructor implementation for your Java class; otherwise, it will show the **implicit super constructor AbstractRuntime() is undefined for default constructor** error. Right-click on the class and go to **Source | Generate Constructors from Superclass**. The following is what the explicit constructor looks like for your custom Java class:

   ```
   public CustomWebScriptRuntime(RuntimeContainer container) {
       super(container);
   }
   ```

4. Each time, a new instance of web script runtime should be created and the `executeScript()` method should be invoked, whose generic implementation is provided in the `AbstractRuntime` class.

This is how you can create a custom implementation for web script runtime.

 You should trace through the complete implementation of `org.springframework.extensions.webscripts.servlet.WebScriptServletRuntime`, which will help you to understand the out-of-the-box implementation of web script runtime. Also, debug through `org.springframework.extensions.webscripts.servlet.WebScriptServlet`, which shows you how to use web script runtime to execute web scripts. This will give you an idea of how to provide the implementation for the required methods in order to create the custom web script runtime.

The custom implementation of a web script container

The web script container plays a key role in executing web scripts. The repository container works behind the scenes to execute repository web scripts at the Alfresco end. It would be interesting to know how to have a custom implementation for the web script container. Let's take a look at the service provider interface available in the out-of-the-box web script framework implementation to implement a web script container.

The `org.springframework.extensions.webscripts.Container` interface available in `spring-webscripts-*.jar` is the key interface that declares the core methods required to be implemented by any web script container. There is an additional set of methods declared in the `org.springframework.extensions.webscripts.RuntimeContainer` interface that also needs to be implemented for a web script container. `RuntimeContainer` basically extends the `Container` interface. In brief, the web script container class must implement `org.springframework.extensions.webscripts.RuntimeContainer`. In the web script framework in Alfresco, in order to simplify the development, there is an abstract class implementation provided, `org.springframework.extensions.webscripts.AbstractRuntimeContainer`. This abstract class implements the `RuntimeContainer` interface and provides the implementation for the methods defined in the `RuntimeContainer` and `Container` interfaces. You will see that the majority of the methods from these two interfaces are provided with their implementation in this class. It makes a consistent and generic implementation for the web script container in the web script framework.

Web script container classes have to provide a definition for the remaining methods that are not implemented in the `AbstractRuntimeContainer` class. In order to understand what we have just learned, you should trace through the code implementation of the `org.alfresco.repo.web.scripts.RepositoryContainer` class from `alfresco-remote-api-*.jar` and the `org.springframework.extensions.webscripts.PresentationContainer` class from `spring-webscripts-*.jar`.

Now that we have an overall understanding of how a web script container is implemented, let's take a look at the high level steps in order to understand how to create a custom implementation for the web script container. In order to create your own web script container, you need to perform the following steps:

1. Create a Java class that extends `org.springframework.extensions.webscripts.AbstractRuntimeContainer`.

2. You will then have to provide the implementation for the required abstract methods. Right-click inside the class, go to **Source | Override/Implement Methods**, and click on **OK**. You should be able to see the default implementation of the abstract methods that were not provided with the implementation in the `AbstractRuntimeContainer` parent class. The following are the methods you will be required to provide with an implementation while creating a custom web script container:

   ```
   public void executeScript(WebScriptRequest req, WebScriptResponse
   res,Authenticator auth) throws IOException
   public ServerModel getDescription()
   ```

3. The web script container should then be registered as a Spring bean entry in the Spring context file. You can give a name of your choice to the bean ID:

   ```
   <bean id="webscripts.custom.container" class="Fully qualified
   class name of custom webscript container" parent="webscripts.
   abstractcontainer" init-method="setup">
   ...
   </bean>
   ```

Now the question how do you let the web script engine use the custom web script container. The answer to this question is that while creating a new instance of web script runtime, you should fetch the bean from the context and inject into web script runtime. You should trace through the code of `org.springframework.extensions.webscripts.servlet.WebScriptServlet` to see how the web script container instance is obtained and passed to the web script runtime.

For Alfresco repository web scripts, the `org.alfresco.repo.web.scripts.RepositoryContainer` implementation and for Alfresco Share web script, `org.springframework.extensions.webscripts.PresentationContainer`, are used by the web script engine as the web script container.

Custom authenticator implementation

In order to access the web script securely, authentication is essential. The web script authenticator is the component behind providing the authenticated access to the web script. Let's first understand how authenticator implementation is referenced by the web script framework. If you take a look at `web.xml` under `tomcat\webapps\alfresco\WEB-INF` location inside your Alfresco-installed directory, you will find the `<param-name>authenticator</param-name>` entry under the `<init-param>` entries of a servlet, which is basically a request dispatcher servlet for web script execution. A request dispatcher servlet will use the mentioned authenticator while creating the web script runtime instance to serve the web script request.

The Spring bean ID for authenticator can be found under the `<param-value>` tag in `web.xml` under a servlet's `init-param` entries. The Spring bean entry can be found in `web-scripts-application-context.xml` or `web-client-application-context.xml`. Bean instances of an authenticator are created using a factory design pattern implementation. Hence, you will find the class name of the factory class against the bean ID. For example, the following is the code snippet for a Spring bean entry for the bean ID, `webscripts.authenticator.basic`:

```
<bean id="webscripts.authenticator.basic" class="org.alfresco.repo.
web.scripts.servlet.BasicHttpAuthenticatorFactory">
```

All the authenticator-related factory classes implement the `org.springframework.extensions.webscripts.servlet.ServletAuthenticatorFactory` interface and implement the `create(WebScriptServletRequest req, WebScriptServletResponse res)` method to return the appropriate authenticator object. You will find the inner class implementation inside factory classes to represent the authenticator object provided by that factory class.

Now, let's take a look at the service provider interface to create an authenticator object. In the web script framework, to create a new authenticator, the `org.springframework.extensions.webscripts.Authenticator` interface must be implemented and must provide the implementation for the `authenticate()` and `emptyCredentials()` methods of this interface.

Now that we have an overall understanding of how the authenticator implementation is used in the web script framework, let's now take a look at the high-level steps required to create a custom authenticator and let the web script framework use the newly created authenticator while serving web script requests. Perform the following steps:

1. Create a custom authenticator factory class that implements the `org.springframework.extensions.webscripts.Authenticator.ServletAuthenticatorFactory` interface.

2. Provide an implementation for the following method; at this moment, just make it to return `null` to avoid showing any errors:

   ```
   public Authenticator create(WebScriptServletRequest req,
   WebScriptServletResponse res)
   ```

3. Provide a Spring bean entry in a Spring context file for this class as follows:

   ```
   <bean id="webscripts.custom.authenticator" class="fully qualified
   class name for custom authenticator factory class">
   ...
   </bean>
   ```

4. Inside the custom authenticator factory class, create a custom authenticator class that will implement `org.springframework.extensions.webscripts.Authenticator` and provide an implementation for the following two methods:

   ```
   public boolean authenticate(Description.RequiredAuthentication
   required, boolean isGuest)
   public boolean emptyCredentials()
   ```

5. Now, inside the method we implemented in the step 2, instead of returning `null`, return the new object of the custom authenticator we just implemented.

6. In order to let the web script request dispatcher servlet use the custom authenticator, modify the `web.xml` entry for the servlet and provide the bean ID of the custom authenticator factory as its authenticator init-param's value, as defined in step 3.

In order to get a better understanding about what we just learned to create a custom authenticator, you should trace through the out-of-the-box implementation code to see how `BasicHttpAuthenticator` is implemented and used by the web script framework. Here are the filenames to take a look at for your reference: refer to the `apiServlet` entry in `web.xml`, `web-scripts-application-context.xml`, `org.alfresco.repo.web.scripts.servlet.BasicHttpAuthenticatorFactory`, `org.springframework.extensions.webscripts.servlet.WebScriptServlet`.

Custom script processor implementation

We should now have a high-level understanding that the web script framework in Alfresco supports JavaScript-backed web scripts and uses the RhinoScript processor to execute JavaScript-backed web scripts. In the out-of-the-box web script framework implementation as provided in `spring-webscripts-*.jar`, the script processor implementation is `org.springframework.extensions.webscripts.processor.JSScriptProcessor` and is registered with the script processor registry. However, in Alfresco, there is an extended implementation to register the script processor with the web script processor registry in the web script framework in Alfresco. Let's try to understand how the JavaScript processor is configured with the web script framework in Alfresco. If you take a look at `web-scripts-application-context.xml` under `tomcat\webapps\alfresco\WEB-INF\classes\alfresco` inside your Alfresco-installed directory, there is a bean entry for the `org.springframework.extensions.webscripts.ScriptProcessorRegistrar` class. If you are using Alfresco Community 5, this file is located in `alfresco-remote-api-*.jar` under the `alfresco` package. The following is the code snippet of its bean entry from `web-scripts-application-context.xml`:

```
<bean class="org.springframework.extensions.webscripts.
ScriptProcessorRegistrar" init-method="init">
  <property name="registry" ref="webscripts.repo.registry.
scriptprocessor" />
  <property name="factory" ref="webscripts.repo.scriptprocessor.
factory" />
  <property name="name"><value>Repository Script Processor</value></
property>
  <property name="extension"><value>js</value></property>
</bean>
```

The ScriptProcessorRegistrar class is responsible for registering the repository script processor for JavaScript with the web script framework. In the ScriptProcessorRegistrar class, ScriptProcessor provided by the factory class bean ID, webscripts.repo.scriptprocessor.factory, is registered with the script processor registry class as specified with the bean ID, webscripts.repo.registry.scriptprocessor.

ScriptProcessor, returned by the previous factory class, is represented as the following bean entry:

```
<bean id="webscripts.repo.scriptprocessor" class="org.alfresco.repo.
web.scripts.RepositoryScriptProcessor">
   <property name="scriptService" ref="scriptService" />
   <property name="searchPath" ref="webscripts.searchpath" />
</bean>
```

When the JavaScript-backed controller is executed, in the internal execution by the web script framework, the executeScript method of the ScriptProcessor class is invoked in the AbstractWebScript class. If you take a look at the executeScript method in the RepositoryScriptProcessor class, it invokes the executeScript method call to the org.alfresco.repo.processor.ScriptServiceImpl class' executeScript method, passing the initial argument as javascript. Going further, take a look at the scriptService bean entry in script-services-context.xml; there is a default script processor name called javascript. The bean ID named javaScriptProcessor contains the entry for the javascript processor implementation, org.alfresco.repo.jscript.RhinoScriptProcessor. This processor is registered using registerScriptProcessor of ScriptService invoked from the BaseProcessor class, which is the parent class of RhinoScriptProcessor.

We have just taken a look at the in-depth technical details of how the javascript processor is registered and used in the web script framework in Alfresco. In order to create a custom script processor and register it with the web script framework, you need to do the following steps at high level:

1. Create a script processor implementation that will extend the BaseProcessor class and implement the ScriptProcessor, ScriptResourceLoader, and InitializingBean interfaces. You should take a detailed look at how RhinoScriptProcessor has been implemented in order to create your custom script processor.

2. Create a custom factory implementation similar to the bean ID, webscripts.repo.scriptprocessor.factory, to return your custom script processor object.

3. Create a registrar class implementation similar to `ScriptProcessorRegistrar`, referring to the custom factory implementation in order to register it with the web script framework.

Custom template processor implementation

Now that we have had a detailed technical walkthrough on the script processor implementation in the web script framework, it's now time to do some exercise to find out how template processor implementation is done in the web script framework and how to create a custom implementation for template processor. You should now be able to trace through the code to find out how the FreeMarker template processor is used by the web script framework and how you can create a custom template processor implementation. Here is a hint for you in order to do this exercise. In order to understand about template processor implementation, you just need to take a look at the bean entry for `org.springframework.extensions.webscripts.ScriptProcessorRegistrar` in `web-scripts-application-context.xml` and trace through the code the way we did in the previous section; you should get an overall understanding about template processor implementation and details of creating a custom template processor. I hope you have enjoyed this exercise.

Customizing formats

Let's first learn about how the different formats are registered with the web script framework. If you take a look at the bean entry with the ID as `webscripts.formats` in `spring-webscripts-application-context.xml` in `spring-webscripts-*.jar`, it has the entries for formats and MIME type corresponding to the available formats. The `org.springframework.extensions.webscripts.FormatMap` parent class for this bean definition entry, `webscripts.formats`, registers the formats and MIME types with `FormatRegistry` used by the web script container in the web script framework. In order to add custom formats, all you need to do is provide the appropriate format and MIME type entry. If you take a look at the bean ID, `webscripts.formats.IE` in `spring-webscripts-application-context.xml`, and its customized entry in `web-script-application-context.xml`, it has defined the custom IE specific formats. It has changed the format for rss from text/xml to application/rss+xml. Similarly, you can have your customized change for formats. If you plan to add a completely new format and MIME type that is not defined in `spring-webscripts-application-context.xml`, then you will have to create a customized `FormatReader` class and a customized `FormatWriter` class. You can take a look at the `webscripts.adaptors` bean entry; it will give you some tips on how to create custom FormatReaders and FormatWriters and register with the web script frameworks' `FormatRegistry`.

Summary

In this last chapter of this book, we understood how some of the key components of the web script framework in Alfresco can be customized when required. While understanding how to customize, we also went through how these components are currently working in the web script framework. In this chapter, we covered the power of working in open source technology, which opens up the door to having a customized implementation as required.

Now, there is no next chapter! I hope you have enjoyed the journey of learning about Alfresco web scripts. It's time now to enjoy your web script development experience with Alfresco to create amazing solutions as per your business requirements.

Index

Thank you for buying
Learning Alfresco Web Scripts

About Packt Publishing

Packt, pronounced 'packed', published its first book "*Mastering phpMyAdmin for Effective MySQL Management*" in April 2004 and subsequently continued to specialize in publishing highly focused books on specific technologies and solutions.

Our books and publications share the experiences of your fellow IT professionals in adapting and customizing today's systems, applications, and frameworks. Our solution based books give you the knowledge and power to customize the software and technologies you're using to get the job done. Packt books are more specific and less general than the IT books you have seen in the past. Our unique business model allows us to bring you more focused information, giving you more of what you need to know, and less of what you don't.

Packt is a modern, yet unique publishing company, which focuses on producing quality, cutting-edge books for communities of developers, administrators, and newbies alike. For more information, please visit our website: www.packtpub.com.

About Packt Open Source

In 2010, Packt launched two new brands, Packt Open Source and Packt Enterprise, in order to continue its focus on specialization. This book is part of the Packt Open Source brand, home to books published on software built around Open Source licenses, and offering information to anybody from advanced developers to budding web designers. The Open Source brand also runs Packt's Open Source Royalty Scheme, by which Packt gives a royalty to each Open Source project about whose software a book is sold.

Writing for Packt

We welcome all inquiries from people who are interested in authoring. Book proposals should be sent to author@packtpub.com. If your book idea is still at an early stage and you would like to discuss it first before writing a formal book proposal, contact us; one of our commissioning editors will get in touch with you.

We're not just looking for published authors; if you have strong technical skills but no writing experience, our experienced editors can help you develop a writing career, or simply get some additional reward for your expertise.

Alfresco CMIS

ISBN: 978-1-78216-352-7   Paperback: 272 pages

Everything you need to know to start coding integrations with a content management server such as Alfresco in a standard way

1. Understand what is unique about Alfresco's CMIS implementation and put your learning into practice.

2. Talk to content management servers in a standard way with HTTP, XML, JSON, and CMIS.

3. Understand Enterprise Application Integration (EAI) with CMIS featuring Drupal and Mule ESB.

Alfresco 4 Enterprise Content Management Implementation

ISBN: 978-1-78216-002-1   Paperback: 514 pages

Install, administer, and manage this powerful open source Java-based Enterprise CMS

1. Manage your business documents with standard practices like content organization, version control, tagging, categorization, library services, and advanced search.

2. Automate your business process with the advanced workflow concepts of Alfresco using the Activiti workflow engine.

3. Manage your documents with productivity tools like Microsoft Office, Mobile Application, MS Outlook, Lotus Notes, and so on.

Please check **www.PacktPub.com** for information on our titles

Alfresco Developer Guide

ISBN: 978-1-84719-311-7   Paperback: 556 pages

Customizing Alfresco with actions, web scripts, web forms, workflows, and more

1. Learn to customize the entire Alfresco platform, including both Document Management and Web Content Management.

2. Jam-packed with real-world, step-by-step examples to jump start your development.

3. Content modeling, custom actions, Java API, RESTful web scripts, advanced workflow.

Alfresco Share

ISBN: 978-1-84951-710-2   Paperback: 360 pages

Enterprise Collaboration and Efficient Social Content Management

1. Understand the concepts and benefits of Share.

2. Leverage a single installation to manage multiple sites.

3. Case study-based approach for effective understanding.

Please check **www.PacktPub.com** for information on our titles